UNDERSTANDING TIME
The Science of Clocks and Calendars

UNDERSTANDING TIME

The Science of Clocks and Calendars

by Beulah Tannenbaum and Myra Stillman

Illustrated by William D. Hayes

WHITTLESEY HOUSE
McGraw-Hill Book Company, Inc.
New York · Toronto · London

Also by Beulah Tannenbaum and Myra Stillman
UNDERSTANDING MAPS: Charting the Land, Sea, and Sky

Published by Whittlesey House
A division of the McGraw-Hill Book Company, Inc.

Contents

1. *Time Is Curious*

Time is curious. It has no beginning and it has no end. You cannot see, hear, or touch time. It is impossible to pick up a piece of time and measure it against another piece. And yet, time is so important in everyday life that you would find it difficult to imagine a world without some way of measuring time.

Time has another strange quality. You can usually judge the length of an inch. But one hour of time may seem much longer than another. An old Finnish proverb says, "There is nothing more plentiful than time." Certainly this is true when you are waiting eagerly for something pleasant to happen. But when you are enjoying yourself at a party, you would be more likely to agree with the Latin proverb, *Tempus fugit*, which means "Time flies."

So it is impossible to depend on "a little while," or "a long time ago." Man needs a way of measuring time that is the same for play-time, work-time, or just plain waiting-time.

With the aid of a clock, it is easy enough to measure time accurately in our modern world. Many first grade children can "tell time." Nearly everyone owns a watch, and there are very few homes in America without at least one clock. But no matter how accurate it may be, a clock alone is not enough to measure the passing of time.

Just as many different units of length are used to find distance, so, many units of time are needed. It would be inconvenient to measure the distance from New York to San Francisco in inches. These cities are 2,640 miles apart, and there are 63,360 inches in a mile. Therefore, the distance is 2,640 miles $\times$ 63,360 inches, or 167,270,400 inches, from New York to San Francisco!

It would be equally silly to measure your age by the ticks of a clock or in seconds. For, if you are 13 years, 3 months, 5 days, 2 hours, 10 minutes, and 30 seconds old at 2 P.M. on January 1, your age would be 418,615,830 seconds. Of course, by the time you finish telling your age, you would be even older!

The year is certainly a much more suitable unit for measuring your age and especially the age of the Earth. The average clock would be useless in marking the passing days, months, and years. Instead, we use the calendar, which is another important device for measuring time.

Primitive man had neither a mechanical clock nor a gaily colored calendar on the wall of his cave. But, although his life was simple, he did need to measure time. Perhaps it will help you to understand his need if you imagine yourself living alone forever in the great northern woods. What units of time would you really use? Seconds or minutes would probably seem very unimportant to you. But you would need to know how much of the day had passed so that you could leave your favorite fishing spot and be back at your cabin before dark. Centuries or millenniums might not trouble you, but you would want to know what part of the year it was so that you could collect a stock of food before the winter snows fall.

These were also the problems of primitive man. And, although he had no watch and no calendar, he did have a clock. The most wonderful, the most complicated, and the most accurate clock of all—*the clock of the Universe!* For, our Earth, all the other planets around the Sun which make up our Solar System, and all the other stars of the Universe moving endlessly through space form the giant clock which measures all time. And throughout history, man has been concerned with learning to read this clock of the Universe.

2. Day and Night

Day and night is the first and most obvious division of time recorded by the clock of the Universe. That part of the clock which is called Earth spins around its axis, the imaginary line which runs through the center of the Earth from the North Pole to the South Pole. It takes the Earth the same interval of time to make each complete rotation. At any spot on the Earth's surface, sunrise, noon, sunset, and night follow in regular order. This is true because, as the Earth spins, each spot turns first toward the Sun and then away from the Sun.

Life was controlled by this movement of the clock of the Universe even before the Age of Man. Plants and animals respond to the changing pattern of night and day. You can see this for yourself by watching some plants. The evening primrose and the four o'clock are excellent timepieces. They hold their blossoms tightly closed most of the day, but in the late afternoon, the flowers unfold. Morning-glories reverse this order. They open their cups to the new day and close them again in the late afternoon. Some plants, such as the night-blooming cereus, open their flowers only at night.

Animals also are affected by the succession of day

and night. When songbirds greet the dawn, the owl hurries off to sleep, and so does the bat. Deer are a highway hazard at dusk and through the night, when they are foraging for food, but they are rarely seen in the middle of the day. Like these animals, primitive man also was concerned with the search for food, and so it is not surprising that time was first measured by the coming of light and darkness.

The word "day" has two different meanings in the English language. "Day" can be used to describe the hours of sunlight as opposed to night, or the hours of darkness. "Day" also means the length of time it takes the Earth to make one complete rotation on its axis. This is called *a solar day*.

The length of the day differs from planet to planet in our Solar System. One day on Jupiter is equal to less than half of an Earth-day. This means that, compared to the Earth, it takes Jupiter less than half as long to make one complete rotation. A day on Venus is probably equal to 30 Earth-days. And a day on Mars is almost equal in length to a day on Earth.

Planet	*Length of Day*
Mercury	probably 88 days
Venus	probably 30 days
Earth	24 hours
Mars	24 hours, 37 minutes
Jupiter	9 hours, 55 minutes
Saturn	about 10½ hours
Uranus	10 hours, 45 minutes
Neptune	15 hours, 48 minutes
Pluto	unknown

But even smaller units than day and night are needed by man in his daily life. And so, daylight is again divided into intervals by the position of the Sun in the heavens. It is true that the Sun and the other stars do not move across the sky, but it appeared to primitive man that, as the Earth rotated, the heavenly bodies were moving. He used this apparent motion to divide the day and the night. On a sunny day, it is easy to tell time in terms of such intervals as dawn, morning, noon, afternoon, sunset, and evening.

Many primitive people still tell time in this way. It is, in fact, far more useful to them than a wrist watch. Knowing it is 6:23 A.M. means little to a tribe which depends entirely on hunting, fishing, and simple farming. But dawn and the coming of darkness are very important moments.

On the other hand, our busy modern life could not get along with only these uncertain, ever-changing intervals of time. Imagine the confusion in a large railroad station if the timetable listed only "morning" or "afternoon" under time of departure. Even in ancient times, when men left behind their primitive tribal life and began to live in cities, a more exact way of dividing the day was needed.

Since the day is the shortest unit of time which can be measured by using the clock of the Universe, man was free to divide the day in any way he wished. At present, in most parts of the world, the day is divided into twenty-four equal parts or hours. This division is based on the method used in Babylon. The priests and astronomers of that ancient country were very interested in the measurement of time, and they made many important discoveries. The Babylonians used a number system based on 12, so it was logical for them to divide the day according to their number system.

The people of Greece and Rome adopted the Babylonian way of measuring time, and it was passed down through the people of medieval Europe to our present Western civilization. Today, when you tell time, you are using a system developed by astronomers and mathematicians who lived many thousands of years ago.

But the day could be divided into any other number of hours just as satisfactorily. For example, in Laos, in Indochina, the day is divided into 16 equal parts called *gnams* (nahms). A gnam is as long as 1½ hours. And in France, during the French Revolution, the state decided to divide the day into 20 parts. This was so confusing to the French people that two systems of time were painted on clock dials for a while. But since people were forever forgetting whether their appointments were made for old time or new time, the 20-part day was finally dropped.

Although it may seem that the leaders of the French Revolution were just trying to be different and looking for unnecessary trouble when they tried to change the time system, there was a "method in their madness." The number system in use in France, the United States, and the rest of the Western world is based on 10. The French Revolutionists felt that people should use the same number system for telling time that they used for everything else. This seems logical, but ideas which have developed through the long ages of history are not always logical.

Many things which are taken for granted in our modern world would be impossible if the hour were the smallest unit of time. Look at a railroad time-table. If trains could leave each station only exactly on the hour, service would be slow indeed. And imagine what would happen at Grand Central Station in New York City! With about 600 trains leaving daily, 25 trains on 25 different tracks would have to pull out of the station as the hands of the clock reached each hour. And to add to the confusion, an equal number of trains would be arriving exactly on the hour.

For convenience, the hour is divided into 60 equal parts or minutes. Notice that 60 can be divided evenly by the Babylonian base number 12. Ten minutes after five o'clock may be written: 5 hours and 10 minutes, or the short form 5:10 may be used. Ten minutes before five o'clock can also be 4 hours and 50 minutes, or 4:50.

For more exact measurement of time, each minute is divided into 60 seconds. A second is the smallest unit of time. It is equal to $\frac{1}{86,400}$ of the time it takes the Earth to make one complete rotation. Ten minutes and twenty-two seconds after five o'clock can be written as 5:10:22.

But this carefully worked out system of dividing time would be completely useless without a way to measure the passage of time. Clocks are so much a part of daily life, we sometimes forget that there are other methods of telling time. Imagine a world without the friendly tick of a clock, not a primitive world where men lived only by hunting and fishing, but one with large cities, busy market places, and fleets of ships carrying cargoes to and from far-off lands. Such cities did exist before the invention of mechanical clocks. Even 4,000 years ago, people needed to measure the passing hours.

3. Sun Clocks

Although no one in all of Babylon, Egypt, Greece, or Rome ever heard the tick of a clock, these ancient people could measure the passage of time. When man first tried to tell time from the movement of our planet, Earth, within the clock of the Universe, it was as hard as it would be for you to tell time from a clock which had neither hands nor face. All the machinery was there, working perfectly, but it needed someone with intelligence and imagination to find a way to use the machinery.

Lost forever in the years before history was written are the first men who watched the moving shadows cast by the Sun and used them to mark the passage

of time. It may have been the shadow of a lone, tall pine tree, or perhaps the pattern of darkness cast by a towering cliff that caught the eye. Although we can never know who they were, it is certain that in many different places on this globe, many different men discovered for themselves that the moving shadows marked the passing day.

NOW TRY THIS

From sunrise to sunset, mark the end of the shadow cast by a tall tree or, better still, a telephone pole. You can mark the shadow every fifteen minutes or half hour by placing a small stick in the ground where the shadow ends. If the shadow falls on a sidewalk or pavement, you can mark it with chalk. When you join all your marks together, the shadow's path will look like one of the curves pictured here, depending on the time of the year.

Although the shape of the curve is different at different seasons, the shortest shadow will always occur when the Sun is at the highest point in its path across the sky. This is its *zenith*. When the Sun is at its zenith, the time is noon, *Solar Time*. Solar time is *Sun Time*.

If you look at your watch when the Sun is at its zenith, you probably will find that noon, Solar Time is different from noon, *Civil Time*, which is the time used in everyday affairs. There are many reasons for this, such as Standard Time Zones (page 111) and Daylight Saving Time (page 109) which will be ex-

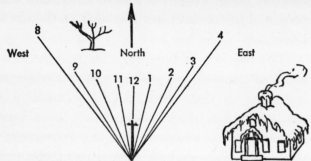

Path of the sun's shadow during the winter months

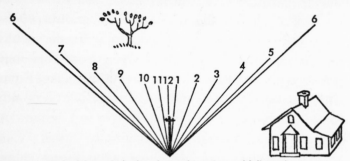

Path of the sun's shadow during the spring and fall months

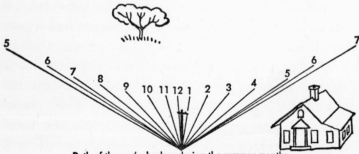

Path of the sun's shadow during the summer months

plained in Chapter 8. But first let us see how we can measure Solar Time, for this was the time which the people of the ancient world read from the clock of the Universe.

The tall tree or towering cliff was the first "clock hand" or *gnomon* (no'·mahn). After a while, men noticed that a thin, pointed object made a sharper shadow than a fuzzy-headed tree. They built stone columns as gnomons so that the movement of the sharp shadows could be used to mark the passing of time.

It is probable that the tall, red granite *obelisk* (ahb'·eh·lisk), known as Cleopatra's Needle, which now stands in Central Park in New York City, once served as a "clock hand" for the people of ancient Egypt. There is a similar long column of stone with a pointed top on the banks of the Thames River in London. Although these obelisks are commonly called "Cleopatra's Needles," actually they were in use about 1,400 years before Cleopatra was born. They were erected at Heliopolis by Pharaoh Thutmose III. It seems that whoever named these columns had a poor knowledge of historical time.

Having a clock hand was a great step forward in the history of measuring the day, but it was not enough. A "dial" was needed. "Dial," which comes from the Latin word meaning "day," was the name given to the face of a clock. It might seem that it would be simple to make a dial by using stones to mark the spots which were touched by the tip of the shadow at each hour. As a matter of fact, this was done in some places. But look again at the pictures on page 18. You can see that the shadow patterns vary with the season. For this reason, the column-type gnomon is not always accurate. Therefore, the scientists of the ancient world began experimenting with methods of improving their *sundial*.

About 250 B.C. a Babylonian priest named Berossus tried using a bowl-shaped dial or *hemicycle* (hem'·ee sigh'·kul) instead of a flat surface. A hemicycle is one half of a sphere. Perhaps he decided to use this because the sky itself looks like a huge bowl turned upside down. For a gnomon, Berossus used a round bead on the end of a pointer which was attached in some way to the top of the hemicycle. No one is certain just how these sundials worked, but we do know that as the Sun "traveled" across the "bowl of the sky," the shadow of the gnomon moved across the bowl-shaped dial. The hemicycle was better than the column-type gnomon with a flat dial because it was accurate at any season of the year. The lines from side to side on the hemicycle are the same as the sun-shadow patterns in the picture on page 18. The up and down lines on the hemicycle are the same as the lines marking the length of a shadow at different times of the day. They can be used to tell the hour.

It is very difficult to build large hemicycles, and small hemicycles are hard to read, for on them the shadow of the Sun moves only a few inches in a whole day. But even with its faults, the hemicycle was the most accurate sundial the people of ancient Greece and Rome had.

The Arabian scientists finally worked out a way to use a flat dial accurately. They made a gnomon which slanted so that the upper edge always pointed to the North Star.

You have probably noticed that globes of the Earth usually are mounted on a rod which passes through the center of the sphere from the North Pole to the South Pole. When the globe is mounted in this way, it does not stand straight up on the table. Instead, it is tilted at an *angle*. When two straight lines meet, the lines and the space between these lines form an angle. Angles can have many different shapes, as shown in the picture on the next page.

If the globe is properly mounted, however, the angle formed by the axis of the globe and the surface on which it stands will always be the same.

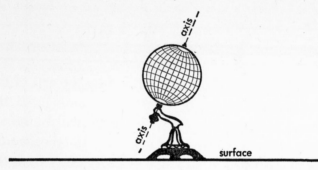

Mathematicians have a special method of measuring angles. Many hundreds of years before anyone ever heard of an inch or a foot, the mathematicians of ancient Babylon invented the system of angle measurement which is used today. This method is based on dividing the circle into 360 equal parts. Each of these parts is ⅟₃₆₀ of a complete circle and is called a *degree*, which is often written as 1°. Each degree can be divided into 60 equal parts called *minutes*, written as 60'. One minute is ⅟₂₁,₆₀₀ of a whole circle. Each minute can be divided into 60 equal parts or *seconds*, written as 60''. One second equals ⅟₁,₂₉₆,₀₀₀ of a whole circle.

An instrument called a *protractor* is used to measure angles. To use a protractor, place the straight edge along one line of an angle with the center arrow at the vertex. Where the other line crosses the arc of the protractor, you can read the number of degrees in the angle.

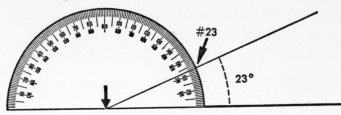

#23

23°

Look again at the angle formed by the axis of the globe and the table on which it is standing. If the globe is mounted properly, the angle will be 66½°. This is 23½° less than a right angle. In other words, the globe is tilted at an angle of 23½° away from the perpendicular. It is no accident that globes are mounted this way. They copy the Earth, whose imaginary axis points toward Polaris, the North Star.

The Arabian system of making sundials tilts the gnomon so that it is parallel to the axis of the Earth and points toward the North Star. The shadow cast by such a gnomon will show true Solar Time on the same dial at all seasons of the year. Most of the sundials that are used in gardens today are made according to this Arabian plan.

If you were to move from Detroit, Michigan, to New Orleans, Louisiana, your watch would still show the correct Civil Time. But if you were to move a sundial from one of these cities to the other, it would be useless. Look at the diagram. You can see that the size of the angle formed by the surface of the Earth and a line drawn parallel to the axis of the Earth differs from place to place. At the North Pole the angle is 90°; at Detroit it is 42°; at New Orleans it is 30°; and at the Equator it is 0°.

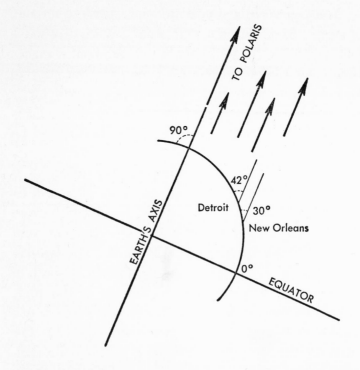

The face of a flat sundial is placed parallel to the surface of the Earth. Since the gnomon must be parallel to the Earth's axis, you can see that the farther south you go the smaller the angle must be between the gnomon and the dial.

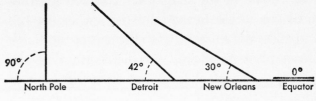

| 90° | 42° | 30° | 0° |
| North Pole | Detroit | New Orleans | Equator |

NOW TRY THIS

You can make a sundial for your garden, terrace, or yard. To do this, you will need: a piece of wood 1 foot square for the dial; another piece about 8 inches square for the gnomon; a road map of your state to find the latitude of your home town; a protractor; a pencil; a compass; a ruler; a saw; some glue, or a hammer and a few nails; a watch; and a level would be useful if you have one.

The gnomon must be cut so that when it is mounted on the dial, the slanting upper edge will be parallel to the imaginary axis of the Earth. Even though you cannot see this axis, you can cut your gnomon so that it will be parallel to it. The *latitude* of any place on Earth is its position north or south of the Equator. It is the same as the size of the angle formed by the surface of the Earth and a line drawn parallel to its axis. (See the picture on page 24.) For example, the latitude of Detroit is 42° and the latitude of New Orleans is 30°. You can find the latitude of your home by looking at a road map. Most of these maps give the latitude in degrees on the right and left edges of the map. If your town lies between two degrees of latitude, use the nearest degree.

Place your protractor on the smaller piece of wood

25

so that the arrow is at one corner. Using the curved edge, mark the wood at the degree equal to the latitude of your home.

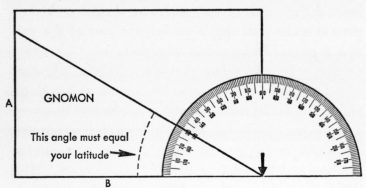

Remove the protractor and draw a line from the corner, through the mark to the opposite side of the wood. Saw the wood along this line.

Draw a line down the center of the larger square of wood which will be used for the dial. Glue or nail

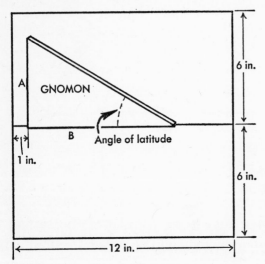

side *B* of the gnomon along this line. Side *A* should be 1 inch from the edge of the dial.

Select a sunny spot in your garden which will be beyond the reach of tree or house shadows. If you plan to make your dial a permanent part of the garden, it should be mounted on a post.

You will remember that the Arabian scientists found that the gnomon must be pointed at the North Star. You could sight the star at night and line your gnomon up with it, but it is simpler to use a compass. Place the sundial so that the 1-inch line between the gnomon and the edge of the dial points north. This is called *orienting* the sundial.

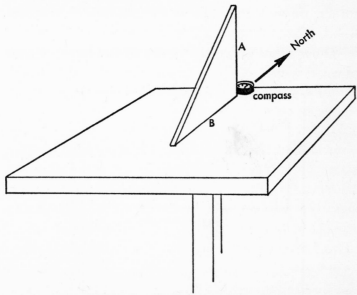

If your dial is set parallel to the surface of the Earth, your gnomon will be parallel with its axis. You can use a level to make certain that your dial is level or parallel with the Earth's surface.

You are now ready to mark the hours on the dial. Before the invention of the clock this was very difficult, because a different dial is needed for each latitude. In fact, accurate dial making depends on so many things that in 1612 an 800-page book was published on this subject!

But you have a watch, and so you can manage without this huge book. The shadow of the Sun always points due north at noon, Solar Time. Your sundial has been placed so that the 1-inch line between the gnomon and the edge of the dial points north. Therefore, when the shadow reaches this line, it is twelve o'clock, Solar Time. Look at your watch, which shows Civil Time. Noon, Solar Time, will occur somewhere between 11:30 and 12:30, or if you live in a place where Daylight Saving Time is in use, it will be between 12:30 and 1:30.

Label the 1-inch line, "twelve o'clock." For one o'clock, mark the position of the shadow one hour after noon, Solar Time. For example, if noon occurs at 11:46, Civil Time, in your home town, mark the shadow's position next at 12:46. This will be one o'clock, Solar Time; at 1:46, Civil Time, it will be two o'clock, Solar Time, and so on, until all the other daylight hours are marked on the dial. Sundials made in the United States about the twenty-first of June can be marked for the hours between 5 A.M. and 7 P.M.

You can make your sundial as fancy as you wish. It can be round or square; you can paint the dial and the gnomon; you can even write a motto on it. Old sundials that are found in the parks and in castle gardens in Europe often have such sayings as: "The longest day must end"; "Make hay while the sun shines"; and, "It is later than you think."

But no matter how carefully you make and decorate your sundial, it may not be quite accurate. It may not be absolutely level. Or you may not be able to make the angle of the gnomon exactly equal to your latitude. Also, although we say that a compass always points north, this is true only for a few areas on the Earth. Place a piece of iron, such as a nail, near your compass and watch the needle move. The needle is made of magnetized steel and is affected by the iron. It is affected in the same way by the Earth's magnetic field and the iron ores in the Earth.

In North America the compass points true north only on a line which passes through the Atlantic Ocean near the islands of Haiti, Cuba, and Nassau. This line enters the mainland on the coast of Georgia and continues northwest through Lake Michigan into Canada. It ends at the magnetic north pole which is located north of Hudson Bay. At any place east of this line, the compass needle is pulled west of true north. At any place west of the line, the compass needle is pulled east of true north.

If, for example, you live near Bangor, Maine, the

compass needle will be pulled 19° west of true north. At Helena, Montana, on the other hand, the compass needle will be pulled 19° east of true north.

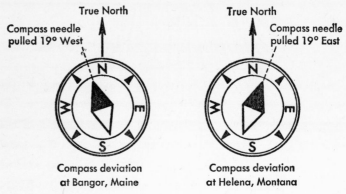

Compass deviation at Bangor, Maine

Compass deviation at Helena, Montana

In making your sundial, you can correct for this compass deviation, if you wish. On the chart below, find the compass deviation of the city which is nearest to your home.

COMPASS DEVIATIONS OF A FEW CITIES IN NORTH AMERICA

Atlantic City, New Jersey	10° west	Phoenix, Arizona	15° east
Boise, Idaho	19° east	Portland, Maine	17° west
Boston, Massachusetts	15° west	Portland, Oregon	23° east
Denver, Colorado	14° east	Providence, Rhode Island	15° west
Kansas City, Missouri	9° east	Quebec, Quebec	20° west
Manchester, N.H.	10° west	Salt Lake City, Utah	17° east
Montpelier, Vermont	16° west	San Antonio, Texas	10° east
Montreal, Quebec	10° west	San Francisco, California	18° east
New Orleans, Louisiana	6° east	Santa Fe, New Mexico	13° east
New York, New York	12° west	Seattle, Washington	23° east
Nome, Alaska	19° east	Toronto, Ontario	8° west
Ottawa, Ontario	14° west	Victoria, British Columbia	24° east
Philadelphia, Pa.	10° west	Washington, D.C.	6° west

If you live near Bangor, Maine, point the 1-inch line on your sundial 19° east of north as shown by your compass. If you live near Helena, Montana, point the 1-inch line 19° west of compass north. Make this correction before you mark the hours on your sundial.

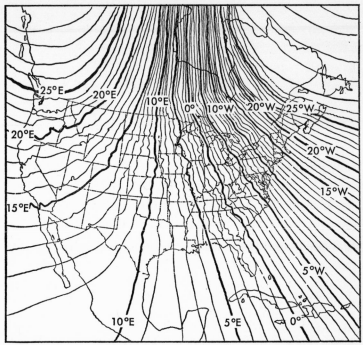

Map of compass deviation

If you work carefully, correct for compass deviation, and level your sundial properly, it is apt to be more accurate than those which are sold for garden ornaments. Remember, however, it will show only Solar Time, not the Civil Time which you use in everyday life.

Sundials are little more than garden ornaments today. But to the people who lived not so very long ago, the sundial was an important way of telling time. The sundial in the garden took the place of the clock on the kitchen wall. Instead of a wrist watch, a man might carry a ring-shaped sundial in his pocket. Even today some Boy Scouts use a pocket "sun watch" which is really a sundial. It has a small compass built in, and it fits into a flat case with tables printed on the cover. These tables can be used to set the gnomon at the proper angle, to correct the compass deviation, and to change Solar Time to Civil Time.

The case of the sun watch is only two inches by three inches. Compare this with the largest sundial in the world, at Jaipur, India. It covers almost an acre of ground and the gnomon is 100 feet high. The shadow moves about a foot in five minutes. At the top of the beautiful, polished brown marble gnomon, there is a small observatory. Unfortunately, it became famous as a "lovers' leap," and so many people jumped from its great height that now the path up the gnomon is closed to the public.

Whether a sundial is as old as the one mentioned in the Bible or as new as the one you made, whether it is as small as a sun watch or as large as the one at Jaipur, it can be used only out-of-doors on a sunny day. Let the clouds form, or the night fall, and the finest sundial in the world is useless. Of course, you can always look at a clock. But what did people do in the past? How could they tell time on a rainy day, or measure the watches of the night?

4. Fire Clocks, Water Clocks, Sand Clocks

There is a very old saying, "Man works from sun to sun ...," meaning from sunrise to sunset. It might seem that before the days of electricity, television, and movies, there was nothing to do but hurry off to bed with the setting sun. It is true that some primitive people feared the night, and right up to the present century, wealthy people in many parts of the world closed folding wooden doors or heavy curtains around their beds to shut out the evils of the night. But in spite of their fears, the people of the past were more familiar with the night than most people of the modern world.

Of course, people today stay up late, but they rarely look at the night sky unless there is a new comet or satellite. Instead, they extend the day with man-made suns. Homes are filled with lamps; the cities shine with street lights, neon signs, and automobile headlights; the country dweller rarely goes out without his flashlight. Even if the electricity fails, there are always candles ready to chase the gloom.

But the shepherds of old, the tribal warriors, the soldiers of Greece and Rome kept their lonely watches in a night which was unlit by electricity. Instead, they studied the brilliant stars sweeping across the sky. Just as we see familiar shapes in the clouds, they pictured people and animals in the stars. The star groups or *constellations* were given names and personalities. Legends grew up around each group. And, in some countries, the constellations were even worshiped as gods.

As men watched the skies night after night and year after year, these stars became their clock. Most ancient people knew the constellation which some called the Big Dipper, others the Big Bear, and still others the Plow or the Wagon. This group of stars is visible in the northern sky at all seasons of the year, and it can be seen circling around the Pole Star all through the night. The ancient sky watchers were so familiar with the way in which the Big Dipper seems to move that they could estimate the time of the night by it.

This way of telling time was satisfactory for the people of the ancient world who did not need to know the exact minute but wished only to divide the night into watches. In Biblical times, for example, the night was divided into three parts: the first watch lasted until midnight; then came the middle watch; and the third watch ended at sunrise.

The "star clock" has certain great advantages. It does not break down nor get out of order, and it is free to rich and poor alike. Unfortunately, it takes years of studying the night sky for a man to learn to tell time by it. And even then, like the "sun clock," it is useless whenever the skies are cloudy. Man needed a way of measuring time that was not dependent on the clock of the Universe and could be used day or night, regardless of the weather.

The simplest devices for doing this were the *fire clocks*. A candle could be notched so that it would take one hour for the flame to burn from notch to notch. Of course, a cold candle burns more slowly than a warmer one, so on a hot day the hours would be shorter. But if exact timing is not needed, a burning candle will serve to mark the passing hours. Also, a measured amount of oil can be placed in a lamp. When the oil has burned, the hour has passed.

An interesting fire-alarm clock was invented by the Chinese. A metal rod coated with pitch and sawdust was placed across the top of a brass bowl. Two cop-

per balls were joined by a string and hung across the rod. One end of the rod was lighted and the fire burned slowly along the pitch and sawdust coating until it reached the thread. When the thread burned, the balls dropped into the brass bowl with a "bong" loud enough to waken the soundest sleeper.

The first "mechanical clock" was probably the *clepsydra* (klep'·sih·drah). Its name comes from two Greek words meaning "thief" and "water." Although it has a Greek name, the "water thief" was invented by an older civilization. Even earliest man must have watched with interest the regular dripping of water— raindrops slipping from a leaf, or a steady drip through a crack in a cave wall. Then about 2000 B.C., some inventive Egyptian decided to use the dripping of water to measure time.

The earliest clepsydra was probably a bowl with one or more small holes in the bottom. This was filled with water which dripped slowly through the holes until the bowl was empty. The length of time it took to empty the bowl could be determined from the sun-dial. This simple leaking bowl was probably the first practical step in man's long struggle to find a mechanical way to measure time.

Once the principle of the clepsydra was discovered, all kinds of improvements were invented. Some were simple. For example, with a mark to show when it was half empty, an hour-bowl could be used to measure the passage of thirty minutes. Other marks could be used to measure even shorter periods of time.

Large bowls, properly marked, could be used to divide the entire day or night into hours. Glass vessels became popular because it was easier to read the water level in a glass clepsydra.

Some of the changes were purely decorative. The bowls were twisted into fancy shapes and even trimmed with gold and silver. One famous clepsydra had a bowl shaped like a face. The water dripped like tears from holes in the eyes.

Other improvements were very complicated. The early clepsydra makers found that when the bowl was full, the water ran out more rapidly than when it was almost empty. To correct this, a double-bowl clepsydra was used. The bowl with the holes was always kept filled to the top, and, therefore, the water dripped at a constant rate into a second bowl with marked sides. As the water rose in the second bowl, a float made it easy to read the passing hours. Sometimes, a carefully carved figure with a pointer rode on the float.

Cleopatra had a clepsydra which looked rather like a modern clock, although it had only one hand. A clever craftsman used the moving float to turn a cogwheel with an attached pointer. As the wheel turned, the pointer indicated the time on a dial.

The improved clepsydras were very expensive, since only the most skilled workmen could make them. And, in the days of ancient Greece and Rome, only the wealthiest men could afford to own them. Most cities had clepsydras in the public squares, and even rich men found it cheaper to keep a slave whose only duty was to run to the square whenever the master wished to know the time.

In Athens, the eight-sided, white marble Tower of the Winds was built to house a huge clepsydra. To run it, a continuous supply of water was needed, and, high on a hill a quarter of a mile away, there was a never-failing spring. The Greeks built a stone tunnel, or aqueduct, under the busy streets to carry the water from the spring to the tower.

Clepsydras played an important part in the law courts of ancient Rome and Greece. Often, the lawyers and judges enjoyed hearing themselves talk and made very long speeches. Without the ever-present water clock, some of them would have gone on talking all day and perhaps all night. So, before a trial began, the judge would announce how many clepsydras would be allowed for each speaker. Court clepsydras usually held 30 gallons of water and emptied in about 20 minutes. For ordinary cases, 2 clepsydras, or 40 minutes, were allowed for the prosecution, 2 clepsydras for the judge, 3 for the defense.

In important cases, the judge might give 6 clepsydras, or 2 hours, each to the prosecution and himself and 9 clepsydras to the defense. A special court officer was employed to stop the flow of water whenever documents were read so that the speaker would not lose any of his precious time. The people of Rome called wasted time *aquam perdere,* which means "to lose water."

Of course, each speaker tried to convince the judge that his case was very important so that he could have more clepsydras. Sometimes, the judge agreed. At one such trial, the long-winded, boring speaker paused for a drink of water. The Roman poet Martial, who was listening, muttered that everyone would be happier if the lawyer would sip from the clepsydra instead of from the cup.

Even though the listeners thought the speeches were too long, time seemed to slip by too quickly for the speakers. Some of the less honest ones were not above arranging to have muddy water or a few pebbles thrown into the clepsydra. This would clog some of the holes and lengthen the speaker's time.

Clepsydras continued in use throughout the Middle Ages. One of the fanciest was given in 807 to Emperor Charlemagne by Caliph Harun-al-Raschid, the hero of the famous Arabian stories, *A Thousand and One Nights*. This clepsydra was made of brass, inlaid with gold, and each hour was marked on the dial by a tiny door. At one o'clock, the first door opened and a single ball rolled out and struck a brass drum. The two o'clock door released two balls, and so on, until twelve o'clock. At noon and midnight, twelve golden horsemen appeared and shut all the doors.

These clepsydras were all made in one or another of the countries which bordered on the Mediterranean Sea. These lands—Egypt, Babylonia, Greece, and Rome—are often called "the Cradle of Western Civilization." The culture of America is largely a product of this civilization, and so Americans most often stress this part of world history. But it is important to remember that other civilizations developed many of the same ideas independently.

The ancient people of India, for example, also used a water clock. Their clepsydra usually was a bronze bowl with small holes in the bottom. This bowl was floated in a larger bowl of water. The size of the holes was such that water leaking into the smaller bowl would cause it to sink in a given period of time.

The Chinese called their ancient clepsydra *Kenglou* (gung-low). It was similar to the water clocks used in the Mediterranean countries, except that its markings could divide either day or night into 100 parts.

Although the invention of the clepsydra was an important step in the measurement of time, the clepsydra is far from the perfect answer. It must have a constant supply of clear water, because muddy water runs more slowly. And, it can be used year-round only in a mild climate, since no matter how clear the water may be, if it turns into ice, it cannot drip through a small hole. Moreover, to be of any value, a clepsydra must remain in one place. A clepsydra filled with splashing water would have little value either to a traveler on foot or to a sailor aboard a tossing ship at sea.

The problem of a portable timepiece was solved, at least in part, by another ancient invention—the *hourglass*. The origin of the hourglass is unknown.

Probably different men working independently in many different parts of the world discovered the principle of the hourglass. Unlike water clocks, which developed into very complicated instruments, the hourglass always has remained simple. It consists of two glass bulbs joined by a narrow neck. One bulb is nearly filled with fine, clear sand, and then the instrument is sealed. No muss, no fuss, no bother! An hourglass will run as long as someone remembers to stand it on its "head" at the proper intervals.

Most hourglasses are small. It is true that Emperor Charlemagne had one so large that it ran for twelve hours. But such a glass must have been heavy indeed! Modern hourglasses usually run two or three minutes, and are limited in use to such things as timing the cooking of eggs. But the hourglasses of the past were used as "pocket watches," for timing the speed of ships, and for limiting the length of sermons. Until the beginning of the present century, it was not unusual for a church congregation to watch with fascination as the "sands of time" ran out on the preacher. At least one clergyman, unmindful of the fact that his hearers were wiggling in discomfort on the hard seats, calmly announced, "Let us take another glass," as he flipped over the hourglass on the pulpit in front of him.

Although these instruments are called "hourglasses," many of the most important ones were designed to measure shorter periods of time. From the era of the great voyages of discovery in the fifteenth and sixteenth centuries, until the beginning of the nineteenth century, sailing ships carried two different sized hourglasses.

One ran for thirty minutes and was used to time the changing of the watch at sea. It was the responsibility of the cabin boy to turn the glass each thirty minutes when all the sand had run out. It was not unusual for him to sing out a sea chanty as he did so. Thus, the men on the watch knew that they were a half hour nearer to the end of their work, and the officers were assured that the boy had not forgotten the glass. During the night watches, the lookout was expected to mumble something in reply to prove he was awake at each turning of the glass. At the eighth turning, the cabin boy would sing out the changing of the watch. Today, the "eight bells" marking the end of a watch is a reminder of the eight glasses which once were used.

An even smaller glass was used to help the sailor find the ship's position at sea by *dead reckoning*. This method of navigation consists of plotting on a map the direction and distance which the ship has traveled. Before the invention of modern instruments of navigation, dead reckoning was the only method the sailor had of knowing his position at sea.

Sailors measure distance at sea by the *nautical mile*, which is 6,080 feet, or 800 feet longer than the land mile. If a ship travels southwest at 12 knots for a half hour, the sailor draws a line on his chart showing that the ship has traveled in a southwesterly direction for 6 nautical miles. Each change of direction is recorded in the same way. But in order to keep such a chart, the sailor must know the speed of his ship.

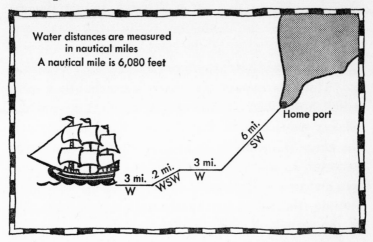

Water distances are measured in nautical miles
A nautical mile is 6,080 feet

Home port

6 mi. SW

3 mi. W

2 mi. WSW

3 mi. W

If you wish to know how fast your automobile is traveling, you can look at the *speedometer*. Sailors in Columbus' day had a different kind of "speedometer." It was made up of three parts: a 28-second hourglass, a log attached to a long rope, and a sailor. The log was light enough to float on the water. If the attached rope were long enough, the sailor could pay it out for one hour and then measure the rope to find the distance he had traveled in that hour. But this, of course, would be an impossibly clumsy method. Just imagine a tiny sailing ship like Columbus' *Santa María* with miles and miles of rope coiled on its deck!

Fortunately, there is an easier way. One hour, or 3,600 seconds, can be divided into groups of 28 seconds about as many times as 6,080 feet can be divided into groups of 47 feet, 3 inches. This means that if a ship travels one mile in one hour, it will travel 47 feet, 3 inches in 28 seconds. If it is moving at 2 miles per hour, it will travel twice 47 feet, 3 inches in 28 seconds.

The sailor made use of this information quite simply. He tied knots in the rope attached to the log at intervals of 47 feet, 3 inches. Then he tossed the log into the sea, turned his 28-second glass over, and counted the knots as they slipped through his fingers. If three knots passed, the ship was traveling at three knots, or three nautical miles per hour. Ten knots meant the speed was ten nautical miles per hour, and so on.

The hourglasses used on board ships in Columbus' day were made by the glass blowers of Venice. These were so fragile that several spares were always carried. Magellan, for example, started his voyage around the world with 18 glasses.

The sand used in the glasses was prepared with great care. It had to be fine, clean, and absolutely dry. One old recipe for preparing the sand called for black marble dust. This was boiled in wine, allowed to settle, and then the scum and the wine were poured off. The process was repeated eight times, and finally the sand was dried in the sun.

NOW TRY THIS

Even without boiling wine, you can make an hourglass. You will need two funnel-shaped bottles

44

(Maraschino cherry or mustard bottles are fine), a piece of paper, adhesive or masking tape, salt, and a watch with a second hand. The bottles and salt must be dry. You can make certain of this by using a "free flowing" salt and by placing the bottles in a warm oven for about a half hour.

Place one bottle mouth down on the paper. Trace and cut out a circle the size of the mouth. Punch a hole in the center of the circle. It is well to use a paper punch, since the hole must be perfectly smooth on each side. Pour the salt into one of the bottles almost to the top. Place the paper on the mouth of the jar. Place the second jar mouth down on top of the paper. Line up the jars carefully and seal them with tape.

Now time your hourglass with your watch. If you use ¾ of a cup of salt, it will go through a hole ⅛ inch in diameter in about 4½ minutes. If you would like to use your hourglass as an egg timer, you can adjust it to 2, 3, or 4 minutes by changing either the amount of salt or the size of the hole. Because your bottles are not truly hourglass shaped, some of the salt will remain in the glass each time, and so your hourglass will not be accurate. But rough as it is, your hourglass can perform its job as an egg timer.

Of course, you can buy an hourglass egg timer in the ten cent store. But if you time such a glass carefully, you may find that it is no more accurate than the one you have made. In a cheap glass, the amount of sand used may not have been checked as carefully as necessary. Also, as the temperature changes, glass and sand expand or contract, and so the size of the opening in the neck of the hourglass varies slightly and the length of time it takes the sand to flow through is different.

Some people like to keep a three-minute glass near the telephone for long distance calls. This can be a real money saver, since there is an extra charge for each minute you talk beyond the original three.

An hourglass is still used officially in the House of Lords of the English Parliament. Instead of a roll-call vote on a bill, the members are allowed four minutes to go into separate rooms, one for the "ayes" and one for the "nays," so that they can be counted. This is called a *division*, and a four-minute glass is used to measure the legally permitted time.

The hourglass in the House of Lords today is simply a part of the royal pageantry of England, a romantic link with the past. Like the clepsydra and the fire clocks, the hourglass played its part in man's struggle to measure time, and is no longer important. Imagine the big row of hourglasses that would be needed in a modern house. In addition to the three-minute size, you would need at least a dozen other sizes. If you multiply this by the number needed in industry and transportation, it is obvious that our present way of life could not have developed until man invented a portable instrument which could measure time precisely.

5. *Mechanical Clocks: Escapements*

The small watch on your wrist is man's answer to the need for a portable timepiece. Mechanically, it is as different from the clepsydra and sundial as your life is different from that of a student in ancient Greece or the Middle Ages. The older ways of measuring time depended entirely on easily observed forces of nature. The sundial was merely a method of measuring the apparent march of the Sun across the heavens. The clepsydra and the hourglass measured time by the amount of water or sand that flowed through a small opening. Clocks, on the other hand, measure time in terms of regular intervals which are produced by man-made means.

All clocks, from Big Ben in the Tower of the Houses of Parliament in London, to the tiniest lady's watch, have four basic requirements:

1. A device which produces the regular intervals— the *escapement*
2. A source of power to run the watch, and a method of transmitting this power
3. Devices to mark the passing of time—hands, dials, and bells
4. Protection for the mechanism—the case

The familiar tick-tock of the clock is the sound of the escapement in action. A basic part of this escapement is the cogged, or toothed, wheel. The use of cogwheels or gears was known to the people of the ancient world. They used such wheels in windmills and water wheels. And they even used gears to turn the hands around the dials of some clepsydras. But in each of these cases, the only purpose of the cogwheel was to transmit motion.

The first requirement of a clock is a device which can produce regular intervals of time. The evenly spaced teeth of the cogwheel in the picture can do this

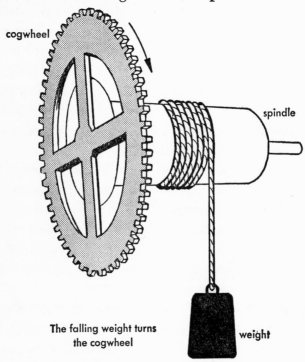

cogwheel

spindle

The falling weight turns the cogwheel

weight

if the wheel can be made to turn at a constant rate of speed. The simplest mechanical means of turning a cogwheel is to attach a weight at the end of a long cord to the wheel's axle. If the cord is wound around the axle, when the weight is released, the cord will unwind and it will turn the axle and the wheel. Of course, a free-falling weight will drop very rapidly, and the cogwheel will spin around at an ever-increasing rate if it is not checked.

By the beginning of the fourteenth century a method had been invented to slow down the speed of the falling weight so that the cogwheel would move at the rate of one tooth per second. The device that was worked out is known as an *escapement* because it allows the teeth to escape one by one. No one knows who invented the first escapement. The honor has been given to many men. Some people believe that Gerbert of Auvergne, who later became Pope Sylvester II, was the inventor. Others give the honor to Pacificus, Archdeacon of Verona, and still others to William, Abbot of Hirshaw. No matter who made the first one, it is certainly possible that the escapement was invented in a monastery. Just as the recording of time had been the responsibility of the priests of ancient Babylon and of many other early cultures, so, too, during the Middle Ages, the monks were the time-keepers.

In 605, Pope Sabinianus decided that the monastery bells must call the people to prayer at seven appointed times in every twenty-four hours. It was the responsibility of the monks to see that the bells rang on time; therefore, the mechanically minded members of the orders were constantly trying to find a better way to measure time.

Although there is no record of the first use of an escapement, we do know that one was used in the great tower clock Henry de Wieck built in 1379 for the palace of Charles V of France. This was not the first tower clock. St. Paul's Cathedral in London had one in 1286 and Westminster Abbey in 1288. But the de Wieck clock in what is now called the Palace of Justice in Paris was kept running until the early eighteenth century. At that time, it was rebuilt completely by Julien Le Roy, who had the good sense to make very complete sketches of the old clock before it was taken apart.

The escape-wheel of the clock was a crown-shaped cogwheel with teeth like those of a ripsaw. Across the front of the wheel was a bar, or *verge* (verj), with two small plates, or *pallets*. One pallet was placed between the teeth at the top of the wheel and the other between the teeth at the bottom. A ¼-ton weight tugged at the crown wheel, trying to turn it. Slowly the wheel pushed aside the pallet at the top, but even as it did, the bottom pallet slipped into place and held the wheel so that it could turn only one cog at a time. A turning bar with two weights called a *foliot balance* helped to control the speed at which the pallets were pushed aside. The escapement could be

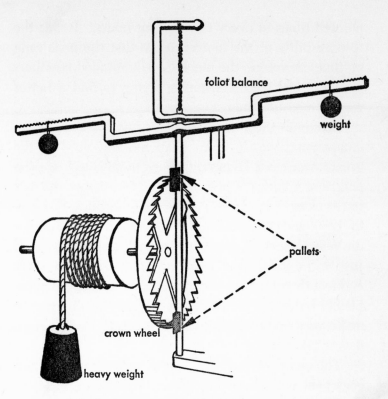

foliot balance

weight

pallets·

crown wheel

heavy weight

A simple escapement with a foliot balance

made to work faster or slower by moving the weights on the balance.

De Wieck's escapement was very crude indeed. The wheels were hammered and filed on a blacksmith's anvil. But crude as it may seem, the escapement was the ancestor of present-day clocks, and a similar device with many, many refinements controls the ticking of the watch on your wrist.

De Wieck's clock was considered remarkably accurate in its day. It rarely lost or gained more than two hours in twenty-four. In fact, when it was first built, it was considered such a mechanical marvel that many people suspected trickery. They insisted that a guard be posted at the tower to make sure that there was no one inside turning the works. As a result of de Wieck's success, similar tower clocks appeared in most European cities. Indoor clocks also became popular, but these were generally kept only in the great cathedrals which could house their 20- to 50-foot cases. By the year 1500, the mechanical measurement of time had become an accepted part of city life.

The first really important improvement in the escapement was the use of the *pendulum*. Galileo, the famous Italian scientist who invented the telescope, discovered the law of the pendulum when he was only nineteen years old. He was fascinated by the great cathedral lamps swinging in the strong drafts and used his own pulse beat to time this swaying. He found that whether the lamps moved violently in a strong breeze, or just slightly in a light breeze, it always took each lamp the same length of time to swing from one end of its arc to the other. This is called *isochronism* (eye·so-crow·nizm), from the Greek words *iso*, meaning "the same," or "equal," and *chronos*, meaning "time."

Galileo also noticed that lamps on long chains took longer to travel over one complete arc than lamps on shorter chains. He used the regular intervals marked by swinging pendulums in timing many of his observations of the stars. Galileo also believed that a

pendulum could be used in regulating a clock, and before his death he drew up the plans for such a time-keeper.

NOW TRY THIS

It is simple and interesting to try some of Galileo's experiments with the pendulum. You will need a cord attached to a weight (a yo-yo works very well) a thumbtack, a ruler, a watch with a second hand, and a friend to help you.

Choose a place to hang your weight so that it can swing freely without touching anything. The center of a doorway is a good place. Tie the cord to the weight and measure 40 inches of cord, beginning at the center of the weight. Use the thumbtack to hang the weight from the top of the doorway.

Start the weight swinging in a wide arc. To time

the pendulum, count out loud the swings of the pendulum while your friend follows the second hand of your watch. It should take one second for the pendulum to travel from one end of its arc to the other. Repeat the experiment, but this time let the pendulum swing in a shorter arc. No matter what the size of the arc is, a 40-inch pendulum will complete its swing in one second.

Now shorten the string to 10 inches and repeat the above experiments. The pendulum will go over and back, or cover two arcs, in one second. If you shorten the string to about 4½ inches, it will travel three arcs to the second. And at 2½ inches, it will speed along at four arcs to the second. If you want to slow the pendulum down until it travels only one arc in two seconds, you will need a cord 160 inches or 13⅓ feet long. It is fun, if you have the space, to hang up several pendulums of different lengths. Start them swinging, and compare the different speeds at which they move.

The swinging of the weight or yo-yo in the experiment and of the pendulum in a clock continues because there are several forces at work, pulling and pushing. One is the pull of the Earth, which is called *gravity*. The law of gravitation states that all objects in the Universe have an attraction for each other. Whether the object is a paper clip, a refrigerator, or a planet, each exerts a force which tends to pull other objects toward it. The greater the size and weight of the object, the greater its gravitational pull. The pull of the paper clip or the refrigerator is so slight that it can be ignored because the pull of the Earth is so much greater. The pull of the Earth is so great that it keeps us on our planet. But if there were no gravity, you could build a fifty-story apartment house several miles up in the air and it would stay there forever because there would be no force to pull it toward Earth.

There is a very old saying, "All that goes up must come down." Once this seemed obvious, for people thought it would be impossible to send anything beyond the pull of the Earth's gravity. But in our modern world of guided missiles, man-made satellites, and artificial meteorites, it is possible to send objects into outer space.

The arc of a pendulum does not take the pendulum beyond the pull of gravity, therefore each time it swings past the middle, or "at rest" point, gravity pulls it back toward that point.

It might seem that once the pendulum reaches the "at rest" point it should stop. But you have seen that this is not true. Instead, the pendulum swings up in the opposite direction. This can be explained by Newton's *Laws of Motion*. The first law states that an object at rest will not move unless it is pushed or pulled by some force outside of itself. If there were no gravity, you could place the pendulum at the top of its arc and it would not swing down. But gravity does pull it down.

Newton also stated that once an object is pushed or pulled, it will continue to move in that direction forever unless it is stopped by something. If the Earth's gravity began pulling that imaginary apartment house in the sky, it would soon be stopped very effectively by the Earth itself. But in the case of the pendulum, the cord keeps it from plunging all the way down to the Earth. And, since nothing is blocking it, it continues on its path toward the other end of the arc. When the pendulum reaches a point where the pull of gravity is greater than the forces pulling it outward, the pendulum swings back down.

If there were no other forces to stop it, the pendulum could go on swinging forever once it was placed in motion. However, the pendulum is stopped, slowly but surely, by *friction*. There is the friction caused by the rod rubbing against the pivot from which it hangs and the friction caused by the pen-

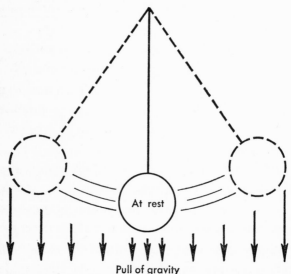

Pull of gravity

dulum bumping continually against the molecules of air through which it swings.

When you use a playground swing, you are part of a pendulum. Pump until you are swinging high, and then let the swing move freely. You will travel very fast. When you are swinging high, you may move along an arc as much as 17 feet long. And, you must do this in the same length of time it takes you to cover a 2-foot arc when you are swinging gently. If you do not pump occasionally, friction will bring you to a complete stop.

The information gained about pendulums was used by many different scientists working independently in different countries. Among the successful inventors of pendulum clocks were Christian Huygens, a famous Dutch mathematician, and Robert Hooke, a great English inventor, who made many important discoveries in astronomy and mathematics.

The first pendulum clocks were made with a crown and verge escapement similar to the one in de Wieck's clock, but a pendulum was used as a regulator in place of the balance. The new clocks were so much more accurate that most of the older clocks were rebuilt with pendulums.

In 1676, Robert Hooke invented the *anchor escapement*. With only a few minor changes, this is the escapement used today on pendulum clocks. In the pictures you can see that an anchor-shaped verge with two pallets is fitted over the teeth of the escape-wheel. The verge moves like a seesaw. As the pendulum swings to the left, it lifts the left-hand pallet, allowing the wheel to move. As a tooth slips past the pallet, the clock "ticks." When the pendulum swings to the right, the left-hand pallet falls into place, stopping the movement of the escape-wheel and the clock "tocks." Each time a pallet slips past a tooth, it gives a little push to the pendulum so that it continues to swing, in this way overcoming the tendency of friction to gradually stop the pendulum.

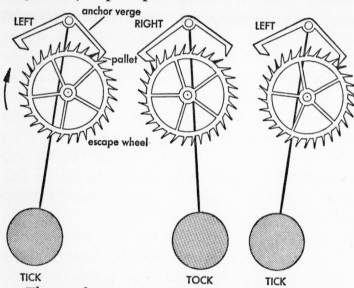

The anchor-escapement pendulum clocks were certainly very accurate compared with older ways of measuring time. But just as a change in temperature interfered with the working of the clepsydra and the hourglass, it also affected pendulums. The early pendulums had a single metal rod with a metal disk at the end. To change the length of the pendulum, the disk could be moved upward or downward a very slight distance by a screw at the bottom. The owner could regulate the clock so that it would go a little faster or slower by tightening or loosening the screw. Once the screw was set, the beat of the pendulum was supposed to remain constant.

Unfortunately, metal expands, or becomes larger, when it is warm and contracts, or becomes smaller, when it is cold. As the experiment with the pendulum showed, the period of time the pendulum takes to travel one arc depends on the length of the pendulum rod. So, if the day is warm, a single-rod pendulum clock will run slower. On a cold day it will run faster.

Imagine that on a very hot day it takes a one-second pendulum $\frac{1}{200}$ of a second longer to travel across its arc. In one minute the clock will lose 60 times $\frac{1}{200}$, or $\frac{3}{10}$ of one second. In one hour it will lose 60 times $\frac{3}{10}$, or 18 seconds. In twenty-four hours it will lose 24 times 18, or 432 seconds, which is seven minutes and twelve seconds!

John Harrison, an Englishman who started out as a carpenter and then changed to clockmaking, found a solution to this problem. He invented the *grid pendulum* which makes use of the fact that different metals expand at different rates. The pictures show the effect of temperature change on a single-rod pendulum and on a simplified grid pendulum. Most grids have many more rods, or strips, but they all work the same way. The white rods are made of brass and expand almost twice as much as the black rods, which

are made of steel. These pictures greatly exaggerate
the change in length so that you can see what happens. The actual change is so slight it cannot be
seen with the naked eye.

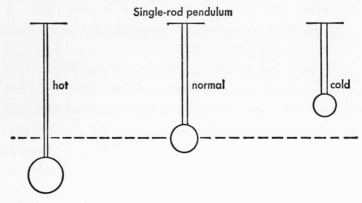

Single-rod pendulum

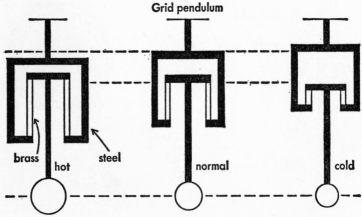

Grid pendulum

Pendulums, no matter how accurate they may be,
are hardly suited for use in watches. The shortest
pendulum generally used in a clock is about ten inches,
and it travels across its arc two times a second. A bit

too large for the pocket or wrist! And while it is possible for a pendulum clock to be moved from one table to another without its stopping, it is not difficult to imagine what would happen to the swing of the pendulum if the clock were strapped to your wrist. A truly portable timepiece needs a different mechanism to measure regular intervals.

Among the earliest watchmakers was Peter Henlein, a locksmith of Nuremberg, Germany. Sometime about 1500, he began to make small clocks and watches. Originally, they were probably drum-shaped, but later, an oval shape became popular. These watches are known as *Nuremberg Eggs*.

The first watches used the same escapement, crown wheel, verge, and balance as de Wieck's tower clock. And they were just about as accurate! An hour or two loss or gain per day was to be expected. There is a wonderful description of a later, but equally unreliable, watch in Charles Dickens' book, *Dombey and Son:*

"Put it back half an hour every morning and about another quarter towards afternoon, and it's a watch that'll do you credit."

The Nuremberg Eggs and all the other watches which were made during the next 150 years were really just ornaments and toys for the rich. Mary Queen of Scots had a watch shaped like a skull. She could open the hinged jaw to look at the dial. Her rival, Queen Elizabeth of England, had a complete set of watches in different colors to match her dresses.

After the pendulum came into use, clocks became more accurate, and the watchmakers, too, tried to improve their product. It was found that a stiff hog's hair, or bristle, could be used to regulate a watch. The hair was soon replaced by a thin, steel spring. This *hairspring* was made in the form of a flat coil. One end of the spring was attached to the axle of a freely moving flywheel. In a watch this is called the *balance wheel*. The other end of the spring was attached to the fixed plate on which all the parts of the watch were mounted.

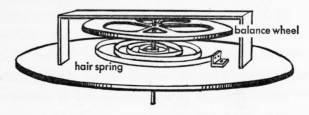

When the spring is loosely coiled so that it does not move, it is "at rest," just as the pendulum is at rest when it is hanging straight down. As the spring is wound tighter, the balance wheel turns. When the spring is tight, it begins to uncoil, turning the balance wheel in the opposite direction. Like the pendulum, once the spring reaches its "at rest" position, it does not stop. Instead, it continues to uncoil itself until it is too loose and so starts to coil again. If you look inside a watch, almost the first thing that you will notice is the balance wheel busily twirling back and forth.

Robert Hooke found that the hairspring, like the pendulum, is isochronous. It will always uncoil and recoil in the same interval of time. The turning balance, like the swinging pendulum, lifts and lowers the pallets of the anchor-shaped verge so that only one tooth on the escape-wheel can pass at a time.

The motion of the swinging pendulum and of the coiling and uncoiling spring is called *vibration*. And it is vibration which regulates the escapement of all clocks. Electric clocks usually do not have hairsprings or pendulums. The vibration to regulate the escapement comes from the electricity itself.

Two types of electric current are used commercially. D.C., or direct current, flows continually in one direction. A.C., or alternating current, flows in one direction for a brief interval and then in the opposite direction for the same interval. In the United States, an interval of $\frac{1}{120}$ of a second is commonly used. To produce 60-cycle alternating current, the electricity must flow in each direction sixty times in one second. The escapement of an electric clock set for 60-cycle A.C. is regulated by sixty vibrations per second.

Sixty vibrations per second is fast compared with one vibration per second of a pendulum clock, but it is very slow indeed when compared with the 100,000 vibrations per second of the *quartz-crystal clocks*. The quartz used in these clocks is the same as the bits of shining quartz crystal which you have probably collected. A very large crystal is cut into the shape of a flat plate. When an electric current is used, the quartz will expand or contract. If alternating current is used, the quartz will expand and contract or vibrate at regular intervals. The vibration interval of a quartz crystal is $\frac{1}{100,000}$ of a second. These rapid vibrations are counted by electronic devices.

Quartz-crystal clocks are not for home use. They are used in official time observatories, such as the one in Greenwich, England, and the one in Washington, D.C. They are bulky and expensive and must be mounted in special rooms where temperature changes and moisture content are carefully controlled. These rooms are never entered except to make repairs. The quartz-crystal clocks in the Naval Observatory in Washington, D.C., are placed in a pit room, deep in the ground. They can be seen through an upside-down periscope. The dials recording the time are located in another part of the building.

The most modern clock of all, the *atomic clock*, also uses vibrations to measure the passage of time. The atomic clock built at the Massachusetts Institute of Technology, in Cambridge, Massachusetts, is regulated by the vibration rate of the caesium (see'·zih·um) atom, which is 9,000 million times each second. Caesium is a metal which is often used in making radio tubes. The M.I.T. clock, called an *atomichron* (uh·tom'·ih·krahn), is hardly a household clock. It weighs 500 pounds and cost about $50,000 to build. But American watchmakers are trying to cut down the weight and cost of atomic clocks and are working on an atomic wrist watch. The atomichron is so accurate that it will lose or gain only one second in 30,000 years! Man has certainly come a long way from the two-hour error of de Wieck's clock.

A tower clock, like Big Ben in London, is regulated by one vibration in two seconds. The pendulum on a grandfather clock vibrates once in one second. The hairspring in your wrist watch vibrates five times every second. Sixty vibrations per second regulate your electric clock. The quartz-crystal clocks in Washington count a vibration of one hundred thousand times each second, and the atomichron is regulated by nine thousand million vibrations per second.

But no matter how great or how small the number of vibrations, no matter how complicated or simple the works may be, no one of these clocks could run without some source of power to start the vibrations and keep them going.

6. Mechanical Clocks: Power, Dials, and Cases

Almost everyone has heard about some famous man who began his business career in the "good old days" by selling newspapers. A more unusual job for an ambitious boy with powerful muscles who wanted a guaranteed weekly income was the winding of steeple clocks. All he had to do was climb the hundreds of steps to the top of a tower and then hoist a couple of one-ton weights from the basement to the tip of the steeple. Of course, some of the weights were a bit lighter, but then again, others, like the one in Big Ben in London, were much heavier.

You will remember that the simplest mechanical way to turn a cogwheel is to attach a weight on a long cord to the axle of the wheel (see page 48). When the cord is wound around the axle and the weight is released, the falling weight will turn the cogwheel. If there were nothing to slow up the action, the weight, when released, would plunge immediately downward. But in a clock it is the escapement that slows the falling weight by stopping its motion as each tooth of the cogwheel passes a pallet. The weight drops slowly, turning the axle, which sets all the clock's wheels in motion until at last, eight days later, it comes to rest in the basement. Sometimes the cables break, dropping the weights with a thunderous crash. Old books on the care of tower clocks suggest keeping boxes of sand under the weights to ease the fall.

Tremendous weights were needed in early tower clocks because of the size and construction of the clocks. Just as it takes far more energy to hoist a one-ton weight than a one-pound weight to the top of a tower, so in falling, the one-ton weight gives far more power to the clock. The first tower clocks were especially in need of great amounts of power. Modern clocks have smooth steel wheels, but in de Wieck's time, and for many years after, blacksmiths forged and hammered out the rough clock wheels. You know how little power it takes to slide one piece of smooth paper across another. It takes more power to push one piece of sandpaper across another. The extra power is needed to overcome the friction caused by the rough surfaces. In the same way, more power was needed to overcome friction and turn the rough cogwheels of early tower clocks.

Until only forty years ago, all tower clocks were powered by falling weights. By turning a great iron handle in the steeple for about a half hour, a boy could wind the steel cable around the axle until the weight reached the top of the tower. Most tower clocks today use electricity. In some clocks, like Big Ben, an electric motor winds up the old weight, which then takes over and runs the clock. Other tower clocks have no weights; they are completely electrified.

The tower clock of Trinity Church in New York City is still powered by a falling weight. Each week for more than twenty-five years, the present clock winder has climbed the lofty spire and turned the iron handle which pulls up the 1,200-pound weight. The church fathers know that electric power sometimes fails, but they are sure that man's muscles will continue to be able to pull up the weight, and that gravity will continue to pull it down.

Falling weights also can be used to power house clocks. *Lantern* and *bird cage clocks,* so named because of their shapes, became popular about 1500. These were small copies of the tower clocks. For-

Lantern clocks

tunately, they did not need ton weights. Not only were the wheels smaller, but there was less friction because they were made of brass by gunsmiths and locksmiths whose workmanship was finer than that of the blacksmiths.

The falling-weight system was clumsy but effective, and you can still find an occasional modern household clock which uses this source of power. The one most often seen today is the *cuckoo clock,* whose weights are usually shaped like pine cones. But if clocks were ever to come off the walls and become convenient little table clocks and wrist watches, a lighter, smaller source of power was needed.

Nearly everyone today is familiar with springs. You probably had spring-driven toys even before you were two years old. Just as the boy hoisting the weight of a tower clock stores power which is released as the weight falls, so energy is stored in a spring when it is wound. When a tightly wound spring is released, it uncoils violently, but the escapement mechanism, which can slow down the fall of a weight, also can control the unwinding spring.

The use of a *mainspring* as a source of power made small, portable clocks and watches possible. But the workmanship was still very crude. For example, the works of a Nuremberg Egg had to be riveted together because, until the latter part of the sixteenth century, screws were not made well enough for use in watches. In order to overcome the friction of the roughly made wheels, a very stiff spring was needed.

While the spring solved the problem of reducing the size and weight of the source of power, it created some new problems. You know that a spring-driven toy runs faster when it is first released than when the spring is nearly uncoiled. This happens because a stiff spring, when tightly wound, releases more power than one which is wound loosely. In order for the toy to run at a constant rate, the amount of power must always be the same.

The first invention used to equalize the power of the mainspring of a clock was a very oddly shaped device called a *stackfreed*. It used friction to regulate the power of the spring. When the spring was first wound, the stackfreed caused a great deal of friction and so used up the spring's extra power. As the spring began to run down, the stackfreed caused less and less friction.

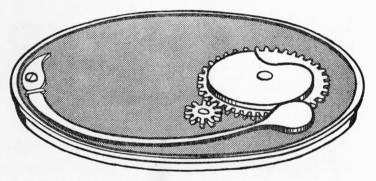

This clumsy device was used in the Nuremberg Eggs and remained popular until Jacob Zech, a Swiss mechanic, started to use the *fusee* (few·zee') in 1525. The fusee was a cone-shaped pulley. Wound around

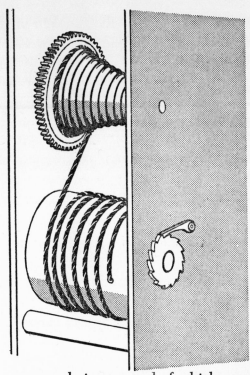

the fusee was a chain, one end of which was attached
to the cover of the mainspring. As the chain wound
and unwound, this device used up the extra power of
the mainspring. The fusee made the watch far more
accurate than the stackfreed, but it still left several
problems. The fusee had to be fairly large. This did
not matter in a clock, but it meant that watches had to
be so thick that they were often called "turnips."
Moreover, if the stiff mainspring should break when
it was tightly wound, the loose ends would whip
around inside the watch and smash the entire works.

About the time of the invention of the fusee, the

watchmakers of England banded together to form "The Worshipful Clock-makers' Company." This was a guild which set up very strict standards of watch-making for its members. As a result, English watches were so well made that they were popular throughout the world. Unfortunately, however, these same strict standards made it difficult for the watchmakers to experiment with new ideas. And, when a way was found to make watches without the fusee, the members of "The Worshipful Clock-makers' Company" were not allowed to use it, but continued to turn out their fat "turnip" watches. People preferred the new, thin Swiss watches, and so the capital of the watchmaking world moved from England to Switzerland.

Fusees are still used in some old clocks today, and also are found in antique watches. But the modern watch is so finely made that there is little loss of power due to friction. For this reason, a stiff, powerful mainspring is not needed. The difference in the power released by a modern mainspring as it uncoils is not very great. But even so, if you check your watch carefully, you will notice that it runs slowly just before it comes to a stop.

The mainspring does not need to be a coil in order to power a clock. Some American clocks made during the last half of the nineteenth century were called *wagon-spring clocks.* They used a leaf spring like that used in automobiles today to make the ride smoother. These clocks were never very popular because they were no more accurate and no cheaper than a coiled-spring clock, and they were larger and more clumsy.

Most people store up power in their watch springs by turning the stem at the top of the case. But your great-great-grandfather probably carried a key on his watch chain which he inserted in a hole in the face of his watch. It took a number of good, healthy twists to wind a "turnip." Modern watches wind with a few, simple turns, and now watchmakers are trying to save you from even this much work. The *self-winding watch*, which is popular today, has a small weight which swings like a pendulum each time you move your arm. The swinging weight keeps the spring tight. It cannot overwind the spring because when fully coiled, the spring exerts a pressure that is equal to that of the weight, and so, the weight cannot push the spring any tighter.

Clocks and watches originally obtained their power from the work of man. But power can also be supplied by electricity. In the electric clock described in Chapter 5, alternating current electricity was used both to regulate the escapement and to supply the power. Direct current is also used to power clocks, but it cannot regulate them. A clock or watch which is run by direct current, as for example, the clock on the dashboard of an auto, has an ordinary escapement powered by a small motor which winds the mainspring every few seconds.

Another source of power sometimes used in very

modern clocks is changing temperature. Here the watchmaker takes advantage of the fact that metals expand and contract with temperature changes. Even the difference in temperature between night and day causes enough movement in the sensitive metal to wind the mainsprings of these clocks.

There is even a so-called "perpetual" clock today. It is the *solar clock*. This has a tiny battery which is charged by energy taken from light. The battery can store enough energy in one sunny day to run the clock for a month. This clock works like the clock in an auto.

If you think that a modern clock is a very accurate machine, you are absolutely correct. Watchmaking has come a long way since the days of the riveted, iron Nuremberg Eggs. One of the biggest problems was to reduce friction. This was done in three ways. One method was to make the moving surfaces which touched each other as smooth as possible. Another was to make the parts so perfectly that they fit exactly. The third was to "oil" the moving surfaces so that they slipped easily across each other. Clocks and watch-makers employed all three methods.

From roughly hammered iron, the clockmakers turned to brass, which can be worked more easily and polished more smoothly. But, for a while, many American clockworks were made of wood. The most important maker of the *wooden works clock* was Eli Terry of Connecticut. Terry was born a few years before the American Revolution, and, as a young man, was apprenticed to Thomas Harland. Harland was an English clockmaker who had come to the colonies and who may very well have been the first professional American clockmaker. His clocks had brass works, but Terry discovered that with the crude tools that were used in those days, he could make smoother, more accurate wheels from hard wood. And in Connecticut, Terry could get plenty of seasoned, hard wood, and furthermore, it was cheap.

Eli Terry was a good Yankee businessman. He figured that if he could make a profit from one clock, he could do even better with one hundred clocks. Terry bought an old water-powered mill, hired workmen and apprentices, and soon was turning out as many as two hundred clocks a year! One of Terry's employees was Seth Thomas, who later formed a partnership with him and Silas Hoadley. The present Seth Thomas Clock Company, which makes solar clocks, is a continuation of this old firm, and its workmen can trace their skill back through Terry to the first real American clockmaker, Thomas Harland.

Many of Terry's friends thought he was foolish to make so many clocks, and they warned him that he would soon flood the country with them and put himself out of business. But Terry increased his sales by reducing the price of the clockworks from $80 to $5, and he traveled about the countryside on horseback selling his wares to the farmers. Because it was impossible to carry many large cases on horseback, Terry often sold the works without cases. Either the farmer himself, or a local cabinetmaker, would then make the case. Before his death, Terry's mill was making as many as 2,000 clocks a year. Such production was still unheard of in Europe at that time.

In order to mass-produce clocks, Terry introduced interchangeable clock parts. This meant that the same escape-wheel, or pallets, or pendulum, could be used in any Terry clock of the same model. It also made repair work easier, since it was now possible to order a new part instead of having to carve one by hand.

Few clocks with wooden works were made after 1840. Improved machinery made it possible to mass-produce brass works, which were smaller and smoother. Today's clockworks are made of steel and nickel alloys. These can be polished to a glasslike finish. They expand very little with changing temperature and are nonmagnetic. The latter is important because a watch with ordinary steel works will not keep accurate time if it is anywhere near a magnet. Even so-called "solid gold watches" have steel works. The gold is only in the case.

Modern machines cut watch parts so accurately that measuring microscopes are needed to check each part. A good watch part can vary from the standard size by no more than one twenty-thousandth of an inch!

But in spite of all this, a watch still needs to be "oiled," or lubricated. The perfect *watch oil* must stick to the exact spot where it is placed and not run all over the works. The oil must not become thick when it is cold nor thin when it is warm, and it must not change chemically, even after years of service.

Thousands of dollars have been spent to find a perfect oil, but no one has been able to make one. It would be impossible to name all the different kinds of oils that have been used. Animal, vegetable, mineral, or man-made—they have all been tried. For many years porpoise-jaw oil was favored in the United States. But today the favorite is a combination of oils. For example, very often chemicals are mixed with neat's-foot oil, which is made from the feet of cattle.

It is most important to use exactly the right amount of oil. In a modern watch factory, one drop of oil is placed on a glass plate in front of a workman. This is enough to oil watches for a whole day. One drop of oil can lubricate 1,066 bearings.

The *bearing* is the hole in which the end point, or pivot, of a wheel's axle turns. It is easy to see that if the bearing were not made of a very hard substance, the ever-turning pivot would act like a drill, and the bearing would soon be worn out. Even the wooden pivots of the old Terry clocks could wear out bearings quickly, and so the bearings were often lined with ivory.

Modern watches have bearings made of *jewels*. These are very hard and can be ground till they are smooth. Sapphires and rubies are used for bearings. Although older watches use natural jewels, most watchmakers today use man-made sapphires and rubies. A 21-jewel watch has 21 pivots spinning in 21 bearings made of tiny jewels. A 17-jewel watch has 17 jeweled bearings. The sapphires and rubies are so tiny that they have no value as gems, but they are very important parts of good watches.

The axle of the balance wheel of a watch rides in a jeweled bearing. But this is not the only moving cogwheel in a watch. Other wheels are needed to wind the mainspring and turn the hands on the face of the dial. All these wheels make up the *going-train* of a watch. Modern watches have as many as 193 parts. Each of these parts helps to make the watch a finer and more accurate instrument.

The going-train of a watch or clock measures time, but man cannot read the time by watching the turning wheels. Dials and hands are so much parts of a modern clock that it is difficult to believe that at one time clocks had neither.

The oldest clocks told time by bells. In fact, the word "clock" comes from the French word *cloche* which means "bell." The idea of "watching" a clock instead of "listening" to it came later. The great bells of the tower clocks were loved by the people, who felt that each bell had its own personality, and so they gave them human names. Later, these names were often applied to the clocks themselves. Big Ben, for example, was named for its 13½-ton bell.

Many curious legends grew up around these great bells. The people of England at one time believed that if anything went wrong with the great bell clock in St. Paul's Cathedral, bad luck would come to the royal household. A family of birds, nesting in the striking mechanism, could stop the ringing of the bell and send shivers of fear through all the people.

It is said that the great bells of Westminster Palace were paid for from a fine imposed on a British judge by the king. The judge had made the unforgivable mistake of dealing too gently with a poor thief. According to still another story, King Henry VIII, who loved to gamble, once bet and lost the bells. Fortunately, the new owner never carried away his prize. That is why, many years later, Tom, the great bell of Westminster, was able to save the life of a soldier.

John Hatfield, the sentry on duty when the palace was robbed during the reign of King William and Queen Mary, was accused of falling asleep just before twelve o'clock. He denied this and claimed he had heard Big Tom strike thirteen at midnight. At first it was thought that this proved he had been dreaming, but investigation showed he was correct. Big Tom had struck thirteen, and Hatfield's life was spared.

The bells on some of the tower clocks were struck by mechanical figures. These were named *jacquemarts,* or *jacks.* Sometimes the figures of a man and his wife were used to beat the bell with hammers. Other clocks had knights in armor or strangely twisted monsters to strike the hours. Stuff and Guff, the jacks on the clock in Herald Square, New York City, are printer's devils wearing the leather aprons of their trade. This clock honors the memory of the famous newspaper editor, James Gordon Bennett.

Stuff and Guff

Very few modern clocks have such amusing ways of striking the hours, but announcing the time is still an important function of clocks. Tower clocks continue to ring out the hour, household clocks may chime each quarter hour, and it is almost impossible to imagine our nation getting started each morning without the alarm clock or clock radio.

Just as there is a going-train to measure time, there is also a *striking-train* to ring out the hours. The striking-train has its own source of power. For this reason, the cuckoo clock must have two weights. One of the iron pine cones runs the going-train, the other runs the striking-train. In weight-driven tower clocks, the striking weight is heavier than the going-train weight, since more power is needed to swing the heavy clapper against the great bell. Spring-driven clocks have a second spring to run the striking-train.

The number of times the clock strikes is controlled by unevenly spaced notches in the locking wheel of the striking-train. This wheel is held motionless by a lever until the clock is ready to strike. If the next notch is near, the clock can strike only once before the lever slips into place and stops the locking wheel.

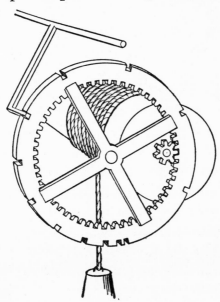

If the distance is greater, the clock can strike more hours before the lever again stops the action. The distance between the notches is regulated so that one more chime is heard each hour.

Some of the old "turnip" watches had striking-trains. At first, these chimed each hour, and it must have seemed rather queer to hear a watch chiming out the hour as its owner walked down the street. When a group of watch owners gathered together, it was said that their chiming watches drowned out their conversation. As a result, later watches were made so that they would chime only when a button was pushed. Chiming watches were very useful in the dark, but it was easier to tell the time on some watches by feeling the raised numbers on their dials. The famous blind-deaf woman, Helen Keller, learned to tell time on such a watch, and today many blind people own watches with raised markings.

Although ringing bells and chimes are a very pleasant way to announce the passing time, they are not very helpful between strikings, and so, a dial and an hour hand were added to the old tower clocks. Since these clocks were likely to lose or gain several hours each day, no need was felt for a minute hand. Minute hands became common after the invention of pendulum clocks made timekeeping more accurate. Today's fine watches often have a third hand to mark the passing seconds, and their dials are painted with luminous paint for use in the dark.

Tower clocks today are most often made with four

faces. There is an interesting three-faced clock in the old Dutch Reformed Church in New Paltz, New York. According to legend, the citizens to the north, east, and south of the church all contributed willingly to the fund for building the clock. Those who lived across the river, on the west side, did not help. When the clock was put in place, only three faces were provided. A blank tower wall looks out over the west. Some years later, this clock became the star witness at a murder trial. The defendant and a friend claimed that they happened to look at the clock on the church tower at the exact time the crime was committed and that they were then on the western bank of the river. Since the clock has no western face, the man was found guilty.

Tower clock faces may be as large as 40 feet in diameter. The hands are usually carved from pine, which is strong and light. Metal hands were formerly used, but these could be bent by a high wind and often needed to be replaced. One great improvement in modern tower clocks from the point of view of the repairman, is a small door in the face of the clock. This makes it easier to adjust or replace the hands. On very old tower clocks, it is still necessary to sling a bosun's chair over the top of the tower and hoist the repairman up to the face of the clock.

Tower clock hands must be reset whenever the clock stops. Failure of electric power and ice forming on the hands are frequent causes of trouble. But it is a flock of starlings which makes life miserable

each winter for the custodian of the City Hall at Stamford, Connecticut. Masses of birds perch on the hands of the clock and stop it. After shooing the birds and resetting the hands several times, the custodian generally gets angry and stops the clock at half past six. This is a most unsatisfactory time for roosting! When the birds finally give up and find other homes, the clock is again put into operation.

One very fascinating clock which is made these days appears to be all hands. The hands are mounted on a clear sheet of glass and no works are visible. These "mystery clocks" actually have very tiny watch movements inside the hands. The large hands are so delicately balanced that the tiny works can move them easily.

The *cases* which hold watch or clockworks are as fascinating as the movements themselves. A watch case must be as nearly dust proof as possible, for a tiny speck of dust can stop the delicate works. It is also important that the watch case be as waterproof as possible. One of the eighteenth century improvements was the addition of a *crystal*. Before that time, watch hands were exposed and needed to be replaced frequently because they would rust or break.

Watches and clocks have been made in every imaginable size and shape. Early American clock cases were sometimes made in the form of an arched church door with steeples on either side. A popular shape for a wall clock was the banjo, with the dial in the round part and the pendulum in the long tail.

Sometimes the pendulum was outside of the case and you could see it swinging back and forth. This was called a "wag-on-the-wall."

The skull watch was once a very popular form, but there were many other shapes used, such as crosses, musical instruments, and shells. It is sometimes said that because antique watches kept poor time they were regarded merely as ornaments and so were highly decorated. But the modern, accurate watch is often just as fancy. Women's watches studded with diamonds and set in fabulous bracelets are advertised every day. Men's watches are simpler, but even these may have gems to replace the numbers on the dials.

Clocks and watches have been made part of many odd objects. They were put into snuffboxes, into music boxes, and even into the heads of canes. Although the greatest number of watches today are made to be worn on the wrist, it is not unusual to see ring watches, cuff-link watches, and money-clip watches. The wrist watch did not become common until after World War I. Before that, most people laughed at a man who wore a wrist watch. During the war, however, when the officers found wrist watches very convenient, they set a new style, and pocket watches soon went out of fashion.

Not all clocks are used to tell the hour. Clockworks are used in metronomes to set the beat for music. The purpose of the clock on the lock of the bank vault is to protect your money. Once the heavy steel door is swung closed at night, it cannot be opened, even with the combination. At the proper time the following morning, the clock mechanism releases the night lock. Stove clocks can be set to turn the stove on and off at the proper time and cook a meal even though no one is in the house. Clockworks also can defrost refrigerators while the family sleeps.

The pocket *stop watch* plays an important part in many sports events. It has no hour hand, and the minute hand moves around a tiny dial. The big sweeping hand on the main dial measures seconds. This type of watch is started and stopped by pressing the stem. Large wall stop watches are used to measure the quarters of basketball games and other sports contests. Most stop watches measure ⅕-second intervals, but there are special ones made which can measure even shorter periods of time.

Many telephone companies provide a "talking clock." Dial the correct number, and a voice tells the exact time. Until a few years ago, line operators answered these calls, but today three revolving strips of movie sound film are used. A narrow beam of light shines onto a photoelectric cell connected to the first strip, or *hour strip*, which then states: "At the tone the time will be one...." The beam moves on to the *minute strip*, which adds: "twenty-three...," and finally to the *second strip:* "and ten seconds." The mechanism is controlled by a quartz-crystal clock, which is accurate to one millionth of a second. So important is time in our modern civilization that the telephone time service in New York City alone answers about eighty-five thousand calls a day.

Talking clocks, striking clocks, clocks with two hands or three hands are all important parts of "telling time." But telling time by the seconds, minutes, and hours is not enough. You would find it very difficult to write the year in terms of hours. There are about 8,766 hours in each year. Multiply 8,766 by the number of years since the birth of Christ and you will see how clumsy it would be to write the date this way. Clocks and watches are fine for measuring the hours, but a different "yardstick" is needed to measure the years.

7. Measuring the Year

Man was aware of day and night as units of time long before he felt the need to divide them into hours, minutes, and seconds. In the same way, he knew the changing seasons many centuries before he used the year as a measure.

Earliest man lived mostly by hunting. He added berries, fruits, and grains to his diet only when he happened to find them. As long as animals and wild food plants were plentiful, it was not necessary to worry very much about the seasons. But gradually, for many different reasons, the wild beasts and wild berries and grains were not enough. Man gave up his roaming life and settled down to become a farmer.

Whenever primitive man turned to farming for his main supply of food, he was forced to learn many new things in order to survive. He had to know when to plant seed, when to harvest, when to store food for the period of no harvest. And in learning these things, man took a giant step along the road to modern civilization. The farmers' calendar of seasons was a first step in the survey of time, just as the measurement of his fields was a first step in the survey of space.

Calendars are so common today that people take

them for granted. It is simple enough for us to count the days or the weeks until the coming of spring. If you are planting a garden, the seed package will tell you the date when you can safely put the seeds into the ground. The calendar on the wall will tell you when that date has arrived. But for primitive people, whose lives were an uncounted and seemingly uncountable series of days and nights, the keeping of a calendar was magic.

Only the wisest men of the tribe could be trusted with such work. Lesser men were happy to share their harvest with those who could tell them when to plant. Since the wisest men were usually the "witch doctors" or "priests" of the tribe, the making and keeping of the calendar became a religious responsibility.

Except near the Equator, the farmers' life is controlled by four main seasons: spring—the planting season; summer—the growing and early harvest season; fall—the main harvest season; and winter—the time of no harvest. There have been many poetic ways of describing these seasons. Spring has been called "cherry blossom time," or "the time of the cry of the migrating crane." American Indian legends speak of winter as the "great gray wolf of famine stalking the Earth."

For the farmers, seasons can best be described in terms of the weather, especially the temperature. And the temperature in a given place is determined in part by the amount of sunshine that place receives.

If the axis of the Earth always formed a right angle

with the rays of the Sun, the length of the day and night would never change. Each would be exactly twelve hours long anywhere on Earth.

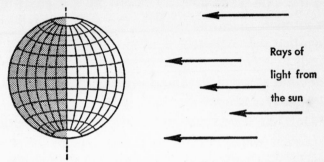

Rays of
light from
the sun

But the axis of the Earth is tilted at 23½ degrees from the perpendicular (see page 22). As a result, except at the Equator, the amount of daylight and darkness in a twenty-four-hour period changes daily. In Washington, D.C., for example, daylight, the inter-

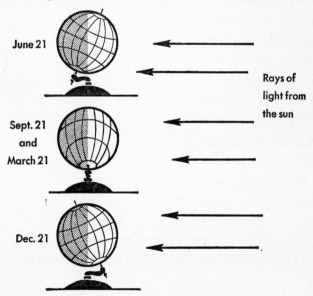

June 21

Sept. 21
and
March 21

Dec. 21

Rays of
light from
the sun

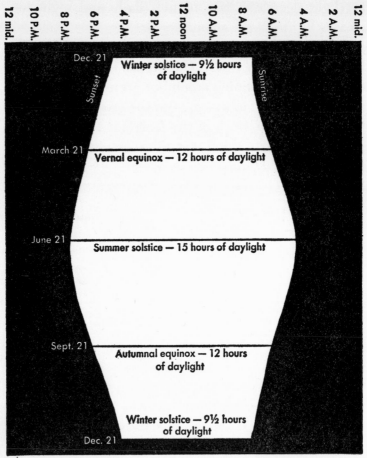

Dec. 21

Sunset

Sunrise

Winter solstice — 9½ hours
of daylight

March 21

Vernal equinox — 12 hours of daylight

June 21

Summer solstice — 15 hours of daylight

Sept. 21

Autumnal equinox — 12 hours
of daylight

Winter solstice — 9½ hours
of daylight

Dec. 21

The changing amount of daylight and darkness in Washington, D. C.

val between the rising and setting of the Sun, increases about two minutes each day from December 21 to June 21. While night, the interval between the setting and rising of the Sun becomes two minutes shorter. From June 21 to December 21, the opposite occurs.

Daylight decreases two minutes daily and night increases by the same amount.

In the picture below, it seems there is always daylight at the North Pole. This would be true if while the Earth was spinning around on its axis it remained in the same place in space. But the movement of the Earth within the clock of the Universe is not so simple. As the Earth spins, it is also revolving in an oval path around the Sun.

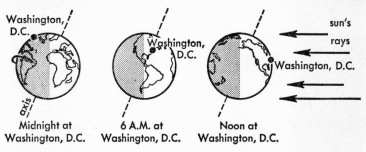

Midnight at Washington, D.C.   6 A.M. at Washington, D.C.   Noon at Washington, D.C.

Even though all the stars, including our Sun, are moving through space at a great speed, since the Earth is moving with them, we can pretend that they are standing still. As the Earth revolves around the Sun, the northern end of its axis is always pointed toward the North Star.

The picture on page 91 shows that the axis of the Earth and the rays of the Sun form right angles only on September 21, which is called the *autumnal equinox* (ee'·kwih·knocks), and March 21, the *vernal equinox*. The word "equinox" is made up of two Latin words meaning "equal" and "night." Only at the time of the equinox, when each spot on Earth is turned toward

93

the Sun for twelve hours and away from the Sun for twelve hours, are night and day equal in length every place on Earth. On all other dates, because the axis of the Earth is tilted, the length of the day and the night changes everywhere except at the Equator.

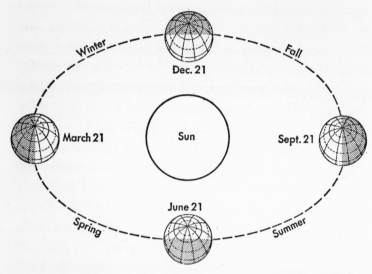

The shortest day of the year, December 21, is called the *winter solstice* (sahl'·stiss). The longest day, June 21, is the *summer solstice*. The word "solstice" comes from two Latin words and means the "standing still of the Sun." On June 21, the Sun reaches its northern limit in the sky, and it seemed to the people of ancient times that it stood still for a day before it started its retreat to the south. On December 21, they thought the Sun paused at its southern limit before beginning its journey north again.

In the Northern Hemisphere, spring, or the planting season, begins on the vernal equinox, when light and darkness are equal in length and that part of the Earth is getting more of the direct rays of the Sun. Plants grow and ripen and the temperature is high during the next six months when daytime is longer than night and the Sun's rays are stronger.

With the coming of the autumnal equinox, the temperature begins to drop and most growth ceases. It is the time of harvest. As the days grow shorter and there are fewer direct rays of the Sun striking the Northern Hemisphere, winter comes.

The early calendar makers turned to the clock of the Universe to predict the coming of the seasons. They believed that the Earth stood still while the heavens revolved over their heads. They found that they could use the apparent movement of the heavenly bodies to foretell the seasons. Predictions were based on the Sun, the Moon, or the stars.

The Moon has always excited man's interest, both because it is the brightest object in the night sky and because it is so unlike the other heavenly bodies. The Sun and other stars seem unchanged century after century, but the shape of the Moon varies nightly as it waxes and wanes.

Many legends have grown up around the "inconstant" Moon. The earliest science fiction stories involve trips to the Moon. In 1657, Cyrano de Bergerac wrote *The Other World; or The States and Empires of the Moon.* This novel related the adventures of the sailors on a ship which was blown to the Moon.

One superstition claims that the Moon causes people to act queerly. In fact, the word "lunatic" comes from the Latin word *luna*, meaning moon.

In spite of the Moon's strange behavior, the earliest calendars were based on it. When counting was largely a matter of keeping tally with sticks in the ground, it was simpler to count the number of new moons between seasons than to count the number of sunrises.

It takes the Moon 29 days, 12 hours, 44 minutes, and 2.8 seconds to complete its orbit around the Earth. Therefore, a moon month, the time from one new moon to the next, varies between 29 and 30 days. A year of 12 moon months would be about 354 days, 11 or 12 days less than our present calendar year. This means that if the year were based on spring planting and so began with the vernal equinox on March 21, the next year would begin 354 days later, on March 10. This would be 11 days before the equinox. And seven years later, the year would begin as early as January 2, obviously no time for planting.

The priests handled this problem in several ways. The Hebrew calendar keepers declared a 13-month year by adding, or *intercalating* (in·ter′·kah·lay·ting), an extra month whenever they found that the grain was not ripening in the proper month. Some Greek and Roman officials added an extra month whenever it worked to their personal or political advantage. In fact, by the time of Julius Caesar, the Roman calendar was in such a mess that January was occurring in the part of the year normally called October. The Islamic calendar still in use in Moslem countries just ignores the entire problem. The Moslems do not intercalate at all, and the seasons do not occur regularly in the same months. In these countries, it takes 32½ of our years for New Year's Day to come back to its original position.

The *lunar calendar* presented another problem. In Biblical times, when the priests first saw the new crescent moon, they announced the new month by lighting signal fires on the highest hilltops. This system was fine in good weather, but a few cloudy nights could cause the new month to arrive quite late. Finally, the priests of ancient Israel adopted a rule that no month could have more than 30 days and there could be no more than eight months containing 30 days in any year.

The Biblical Hebrew calendar was certainly very complicated, and the Islamic calendar had little value for the farmer, but at least these were based on definite rules. Most early lunar calendars were so dependent on the whims of the priests, that in some countries *solar calendars* began to appear. Often, both calendars were used together for many years, and sometimes violent feelings arose between the followers of each type of calendar.

By the time Julius Caesar came into power, the Romans had been using a solar calendar for about four hundred years. But there were still remnants of the old 10-month lunar calendar which legend says Romulus set up when he founded the city of Rome. This calendar began in March and ended with the tenth month, December. Before Caesar's day, two extra months—January and February—were added. Today, we still use the Roman names in our calendar.

Martius	named for Mars, the god of war
Aprilis	named for the awakening of the Earth
Maius	named for Maia, the goddess of growth
Junius	named for Juno, the queen of the gods
Quintilis	fifth
Sextilis	sixth
September	seventh
October	eighth
November	ninth
December	tenth
Januarius	named for Janus, the god of the gate
Februarius	named for the holiday of purification

One of the earliest solar calendars was made in Egypt. The year was based on 365 days divided into 12 months of 30 days each. There were 360 regular days, and each of the other five days was a feast day set aside to celebrate the birthday of a god. The gods thus honored were: Osiris, god of good and judge of the dead; Horus, the sun god, who daily drove the sun chariot across the sky; Isis, goddess of nature; Set, god of night and evil; and Nephthys, sister of Osiris and Set. The Coptic Christian Church, which is the state church of Ethiopia, still uses such a calendar. Of course, the five extra days no longer honor pagan gods.

In the Western Hemisphere, the Mayan Indians also produced a 365-day solar calendar. It was made up of 18 months, each 20 days long. The remaining five days, however, were not holidays. Instead, they were the "Friday, the thirteenths" of the Mayan world, days of very bad luck.

Many early solar calendars placed New Year's Day at the vernal equinox. Even some of the very ancient people could tell exactly when the equinox occurred. For example, in England, about four thousand years ago, the early Britons set up great double circles of stone called *Stonehenge*. When the Sun rose at a point on the horizon between two particular stone columns, they celebrated the equinox. This is a permanent stone calendar which can still be used today.

Unfortunately for the calendar makers, the solar year is not exactly 365 days in length. Since the Earth is in constant movement around the Sun, the spring equinox actually occurs for only one fleeting second. Newspapers usually tell us the exact moment spring arrives each year. And it takes the Earth 365 days, 5 hours, 48 minutes, and 46 seconds to whirl from one vernal equinox to the next. Somehow the calendar makers must take care of the 5 hours, 48 minutes, and 46 seconds that are left over when a 365-day year is used.

The Egyptians may have been the first to recognize this. For, in addition to the lunar and solar calendars, they used a star to measure the year. The most important event in ancient Egypt was the yearly flooding of the Nile River. Without this, the rich Nile Valley would have become a desert wasteland. The priests observed that each year, just before the Nile flooded, the Dog Star, *Sirius* (sihr′·ee·us), appeared at dawn in the eastern sky. They used the appearance of Sirius to mark the beginning of the new year.

So important was the Dog Star in the lives of the Egyptians that they made sure that even the dead Pharaoh would see it. They built a special narrow shaft into the Great Pyramid of Pharaoh Cheops (key′·ahps). And, for one fleeting second, as the star reached its highest point in the heavens, the light of Sirius shone down on the face of the dead Pharaoh.

The appearance of a star, or a constellation, on the Eastern horizon at either sunrise or sunset has been used by many other people as a basis for a calendar. The *Pleiades* (plee′·yah·deez) is a group of stars which has been used often in different parts of the world. For example, this group has been used by the Orinoco Indians of South America and by the tribes of the Solomon Islands in the Pacific Ocean.

Unlike these primitive peoples, however, the priests of Egypt kept careful records. They discovered that at the end of each cycle of four years, Sirius was one day late in making its early morning appearance. From this, they concluded that the year must be 365¼ days in length.

The calendar we use today is a direct outgrowth of Egyptian astronomy. It is based on the *Julian calendar*, which was prepared by the Alexandrian scientist, Sosigenes, under orders from Julius Caesar. To flatter the great Caesar, the name of the fifth month, Quintilis, was changed to Julius. And Caesar's successor, Augustus, had his name given to Sextus, the sixth month. Sosigenes also changed New Year's Day to January 1. This caused December, meaning "tenth," to become the twelfth month.

Sosigenes followed the teaching of the ancient Egyptian priests. He believed that the length of the year was exactly 365 days and 6 hours, or 365¼ days. He took care of the extra hours by intercalating one day every fourth year, or *Leap Year*. This seemed to work very well for many years, but gradually the error of 11 minutes and 14 seconds added up to a noticeable period of time. After 500 years, the error amounted to 3 whole days. And, by the time Columbus set sail on his voyages of discovery, the Julian calendar was wrong by nearly 10 days.

During the sixteenth century, scientists tried to persuade Pope Gregory XIII to correct the calendar. The famous astronomer Clavius had a special room called the *sala del calendaria* built in the Vatican in Rome to prove that the vernal equinox was occurring on March 11 instead of March 21. This was a serious error for the Catholic Church because the celebration of the very important holiday, Easter, must occur on the Sunday following the first full moon after the vernal equinox. The full moon made it possible for people to travel at night to the Easter festivals.

Gregory finally was convinced, and he declared that for the year 1582, the day after October 4 would be called October 15. This seems a simple enough way to make the correction, but when it was announced, there were riots throughout Europe. Italy, Spain, Portugal, France, and Poland accepted the change immediately. England and her possessions, including the thirteen American colonies, did not change until 1752. Russia did not adopt the *Gregorian calendar* until 1918, after the Soviet Revolution, and Turkey finally changed to the New Style in 1927.

Fighting broke out in the streets of the cities of England when the change was announced there. By that time, the calendar was eleven days late. Many people accused the government of stealing eleven days from their lives. Some absolutely refused to accept the change and went on using the old dates. Things became so confused that for a while it was necessary to use both dates on important papers. Even today you will find books which list the date of George Washington's birth as February 22, 1732, *New Style,* and February 11, 1731, *Old Style* (or O.S.). This is necessary, for in the colonies when Washington was born, the date was February 11, although in most of Europe it was February 22. The year was 1731 instead of 1732 because under the Old Style, New Year's Day was March 25 rather than January 1.

When the United States purchased Alaska from Russia in 1867, the local calendar had to be brought up to date. Since Russia did not adopt the Gregorian calendar until 1918, the old Julian calendar was still in use in Alaska. When the Americans took over, 11 days had to be dropped.

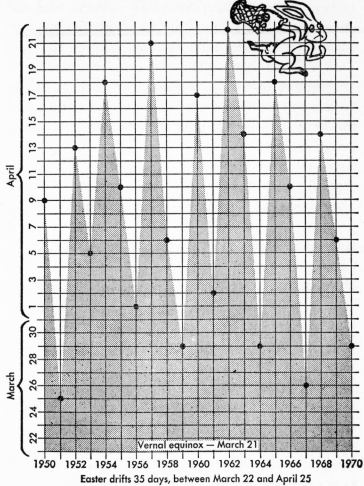

April

March

Vernal equinox — March 21

1950 1952 1954 1956 1958 1960 1962 1964 1966 1968 **1970**

Easter drifts 35 days, between March 22 and April 25

The Gregorian calendar not only corrected the time gained under the Julian calendar but tried to prevent this from happening again. This is done by omitting three leap years from every four centuries. This always takes place at the turn of the century.

1600—Leap year
1700—No leap year
1800—No leap year
1900—No leap year
2000—Leap year
2100—No leap year
2200—No leap year
2300—No leap year
2400—Leap year

With this arrangement of leap years, the *solar year* is only 26 seconds shorter than the average *calendar year*. It will take 3,323 years, or until the year 4905, for the error to equal one day.

The modern calendar is certainly accurate enough for everyday needs, but it still has some faults. The most annoying one is that each year, the day of the week changes for a given date. When July 4 occurs on Sunday, the following year it will occur on Monday, unless it is leap year. In that case, it will fall on Tuesday. This happens because when you divide 365 days by 7 days, the result is 52 weeks and 1 day. leap year, of course, has 366 days, and therefore, there are 52 weeks and 2 days. The same order of days and dates is repeated only after 28 years.

If you wish to know the day of the week on which you were born, you either must find a calendar for that year or count backwards by years. Be sure to skip an extra day for each leap year. If you should wish to know the day of the week on which something happened hundreds of years ago, counting backwards would be very difficult. But you could look it up in a special table called a *perpetual calendar*. There probably is a perpetual calendar in your library. Some almanacs also include these calendars. With one, you could find that the Declaration of Independence was signed on Thursday, and that December 16, 1773, when the Boston Tea Party took place, also was a Thursday. Or perhaps you would rather use it to look into the future and find that January 1, 2000, will occur on Sunday.

Some people would like to change the calendar again so that the same date would occur on the same day of the week each year. These people propose a *World calendar* of 12 months so arranged that each 31-day month is followed by two months of 30 days each. Under this plan, there would be 31 days in January, 30 days in February, 30 days in March, 31 days in April, etc. The day after December 30 would be called *Year's End Day* rather than Sunday, Monday, or any of the other weekday names. A similar extra day called *Leap Year Day* would follow June 30 every fourth year. With this calendar, the new year would begin always on Sunday, and Christmas would occur on Monday.

The World calendar has many advantages, and the people who believe in it are working very hard to have it adopted. But it seems unlikely that any change will take place soon. Although our calendar is man-made, many people think that man has no right to change it. One strong argument is that by adding Year's End Day and Leap Year Day, the Sabbath would not fall regularly on the seventh day, as prescribed in the Bible.

Any tampering with the calendar brings forth howls of protest. Not so many years ago, President Franklin D. Roosevelt moved Thanksgiving Day up one week to give the stores a longer pre-Christmas shopping season. There were so many protests that the change lasted only three years. And Thanksgiving has been a national holiday only since 1863!

Today, many nations use only the Gregorian calendar, but other countries use two or more calendars. An example of a country with many calendars is India. The Gregorian calendar is used for official purposes, such as payment of salaries, taxes, and national anniversaries. For everyday and religious purposes, there are as many as seventeen different calendars made up by local calendar makers. The government of India prepared a new calendar which went into effect on March 22, 1957. This calendar is used by the government to establish religious holidays, but it does not replace the Gregorian calendar.

No one can tell whether or not the people will accept the new Indian calendar. Even the strongest governments sometimes cannot force calendar change. The government of the French Revolution, with the help of the guillotine, forced the people to use the "Calendar of Reason." It had 12 months of 30 days each. The extra five days in the year were called *Sansculotticides* in honor of the very poor people, who were called *Sans Culottes* (sahn·koo·lawt'), which means "without pants" in French. There were no weeks, but each month was divided into three "decades," each having ten days. Feeling was so strong, that France was soon divided into two parties, either for or against the new calendar, and the calendar lasted only twelve years.

Modern man is so dependent on his calendar and clock that he will fight hard against any attempt to change his system of time. But calendars and clocks are not enough. Man needs fixed rules to help him use these instruments of measurement. A few hundred years ago a traveler in Italy could celebrate three different New Year's Days in one year by going from one city to another. And if he went to France and Spain, he could enjoy two more celebrations. This kind of confusion would never do in the busy modern world. Time must be standardized as well as measured.

8. *Standardizing Time*

Time is like a continuous line which has no obvious beginning nor end. For example, when did today begin? In most countries of the world, the answer is at midnight, but this was not always the case. Probably the rising Sun was used by earliest man to indicate the beginning of a new day. Egypt and, later, Rome, both of which used solar calendars, began the day at sunrise. Because Babylonia and Biblical Israel had lunar calendars, they were more concerned with nighttime, and therefore dated the new day at sundown.

Since the time when the Sun rises and sets changes daily, this system would be confusing in our complicated modern world. It is simplest to change dates at midnight, when there is very little business or other activity. But until man had invented an accurate way to measure the hours of the night, regardless of the weather, it was necessary to use the Sun to herald the coming of a new day.

There still are remnants of the old systems in use today. In Israel, you have a choice. The date changes at midnight for those who employ the Gregorian calendar. People who use the Hebrew calendar change the date at sundown. Newspapers and official documents use both calendars. For religious holidays, the ever-changing sundown hour is always used. In Yemen, a tiny country on the Red Sea, the new day begins when a man can distinguish a black goat hair from a white one.

Although man has made his own rules about time, any change is still regarded with suspicion. During World War I, *Daylight Saving Time* was introduced to give people an extra hour of daylight by setting the clock ahead one hour. Many people were violently opposed to it, especially the farmers. Some people still insist that *Standard Time* is God's time and Daylight Saving is man-made time. These people assume that Standard Time, which was not used in the United States until 1883, is based entirely on the position of the Sun. But this is not true.

Suppose that everyday time was determined by *solar noon*. At any given place, solar noon occurs when the Sun reaches its zenith, the highest point in its apparent path across the sky. It is always solar noon somewhere on Earth. Since the Earth is constantly spinning on its axis, solar noon occurs for only one fleeting part of a second at any given place. Noon on the western side of the street is a very tiny fraction of a second later than noon on the eastern side. Solar noon occurs about two minutes later on the western edge of New Orleans than on the eastern city line. It takes solar noon about forty-eight minutes to travel across the state of Montana, but less than two and one-half minutes to cross Delaware.

Imagine trying to keep your watch adjusted to Solar Time. Every step toward the East or West would change the basis of time. Only if you moved directly north or south would your watch remain accurate. Of course, a few steps would not make any noticeable difference, but crossing a state, or even a large city, would make a real difference. So man adjusts time to suit his convenience.

The circumference of the Earth is a circle, and therefore can be divided into 360 degrees. It takes twenty-four hours for the Earth to spin around, so that solar noon occurs over each of these degrees. This means that noon occurs westward at the rate of 15 degrees every hour. In 1884, the representatives of many governments held an international conference in Washington, D.C., and approved a plan to divide the entire world into twenty-four time zones, each fifteen degrees in width. Each of these time zones extends from the North Pole to the South Pole.

Some nations did not accept this plan. Countries such as Saudi Arabia, Mongolia, and Afghanistan make up their own time. For example, when the Sun goes down in Saudi Arabia, it is twelve o'clock local time. Since the hour of sundown is different each day, watches must be reset each time the Sun sets.

Each of the lines in the illustration is a *meridian* (meh·rid′·ee·yan). A meridian is one half of a great circle on the globe which passes from Pole to Pole. Any number of meridians can be drawn on a globe.

For example, an imaginary line could be drawn from the North to the South Pole passing through your home.

When the Sun passes over the meridian of your city or town, it is *noon, solar time.* The abbreviation A.M., for *ante meridian,* comes from the Latin and means "before the meridian," or "before noon." P.M., or *post meridian,* is also Latin and means "after the meridian," or "after noon."

Meridians are numbered in degrees east or west of the *prime meridian.* Just as man chose midnight to mark the beginning of a new day, so he selected a prime meridian to help standardize time. Once it was the custom for each country to call the meridian passing through its capital the prime meridian. Such a system, of course, made it impossible to standardize time for the whole world. At the Washington Conference, it was agreed that the meridian passing through the Greenwich Observatory in London, England, would be called the prime meridian.

The Greenwich Civil Time Zone (G.C.T.) extends $7\frac{1}{2}°$ east and $7\frac{1}{2}°$ west of the prime meridian. The time zone directly west of the Greenwich Zone covers the 15 degrees from $7\frac{1}{2}°$ West to $22\frac{1}{2}°$ West. It includes Iceland and some of the western edge of Africa. When it is 12, noon, at Greenwich, it is one hour earlier, or 11 A.M., in these places. A man traveling west from Greenwich must set his watch back one hour as he crosses into each new time zone.

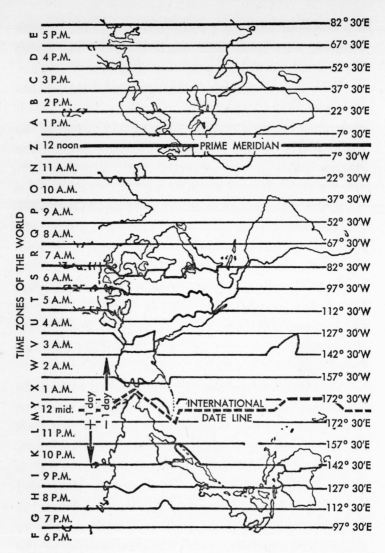

TIME ZONES OF THE WORLD

E	5 P.M.	82° 30'E
D	4 P.M.	67° 30'E
C	3 P.M.	52° 30'E
B	2 P.M.	37° 30'E
A	1 P.M.	22° 30'E
Z	12 noon	7° 30'E
	PRIME MERIDIAN	7° 30'W
N	11 A.M.	22° 30'W
O	10 A.M.	37° 30'W
P	9 A.M.	52° 30'W
Q	8 A.M.	67° 30'W
R	7 A.M.	82° 30'W
S	6 A.M.	97° 30'W
T	5 A.M.	112° 30'W
U	4 A.M.	127° 30'W
V	3 A.M.	142° 30'W
W	2 A.M.	157° 30'W
X	1 A.M.	172° 30'W
Y	12 mid.	INTERNATIONAL DATE LINE
M		172° 30'E
L	11 P.M.	157° 30'E
K	10 P.M.	142° 30'E
I	9 P.M.	127° 30'E
H	8 P.M.	112° 30'E
G	7 P.M.	97° 30'E
F	6 P.M.	

+1 day   −1 day

The time zone immediately east of the Greenwich
Zone includes most of the European countries and
parts of Africa. When it is 12, noon, at Greenwich,

112

it is one hour later, or 1 P.M., in these places. A man traveling east from Greenwich must set his watch ahead one hour as he crosses into each new time zone.

Each of the twenty-four time zones of the world has been assigned a letter of the alphabet. This makes it easier to identify the time zone of any place in the world and give its local time. The Greenwich Time Zone is called "Z." Washington, D.C., is in the Eastern Standard Time Zone which is "R." Los Angeles is in the Pacific Standard Time Zone, called "U." Moscow is in the "C" Zone, and Hong Kong is in "H."

Because time zones are 15 degrees wide, the time is accurate only for the meridian passing through the center of the zone. At the eastern edge of the zone, the clock is one-half hour slower than the Sun. At the western edge, the clock is one-half hour faster. Man has made an "average sun" to use in determining civil time.

In addition to an "average noon" for an entire time zone, man has had to set up an "average noon" from day to day. This is necessary because the Sun does not cross a meridian exactly every twenty-four hours. Since the shape of the Earth's path around the Sun is not a circle, sometimes the Earth travels faster, and sometimes slower. True noon varies as much as eighteen minutes. The *equation of time* is used to tell exactly when true noon occurs each day of the year. Most globes have an equation of time in the form of a double loop printed on them. Almanacs give detailed tables for the equation of time so that you can tell just when true noon occurs over any meridian any day.

Although the Washington Conference divided the world into 15-degree sections, a glance at the time zone map will show you that zone lines do not follow meridian lines exactly. Smaller countries and states find it less confusing to be entirely within one time zone. So the lines are twisted to follow political boundaries. Some American towns, such as Apalachicola, Florida; Stockton, Kansas; and Huntington, Oregon; are located on time zone lines. In these cases, the lines are bent around the town so that the people will not lose or gain an hour whenever they go from one side of the town to the other.

In the United States, the Interstate Commerce Commission is responsible for setting time zone boundaries. Changes can be made whenever it seems necessary. For example, in 1950, the commission changed the line between Mountain and Pacific Time Zones so that all of Arizona would use Mountain Standard Time (M.S.T.)

Military and naval messages which must be sent across time zone lines always use Greenwich Time. Moreover, the hours are numbered from one to twenty-four. With this system, 8:30 A.M. becomes 0830; 2 P.M. is 1400; and 8:30 P.M. becomes 2030. A military message radioed from Washington, D.C., at three in the afternoon, Eastern Standard Time (E.S.T.) would be received in San Francisco at 12, noon, Pacific Standard Time (P.C.T.), but it would be dated

2000 G.C.T., which is eight in the evening on the prime meridian.

Only that half of the great circle which starts at the North Pole, passes through Greenwich, England, and ends at the South Pole is the prime meridian. The other half of the same circle, which crosses the Pacific Ocean, is called the *International Date Line*. Just as it was necessary to choose an hour when the day began in time, it was necessary to choose a line where the day began in space. When it is one minute past noon, January 1, on the prime meridian, it is one minute after midnight, January 2, along the International Date Line. A ship's passenger crossing the International Date Line in a westerly direction loses one day. For example, 6 P.M., January 2, becomes 6 P.M., January 3, when the line is crossed. A passenger on an east-bound ship, crossing at the same time, would gain one day.

Crossing the International Date Line can create strange situations. When several U.S. Air Force planes flew around the world in forty-five hours and nineteen minutes, a little less than two days, their crews lived one night longer than anyone else on Earth. Since the men were flying eastward, they were rushing to meet the Sun and passed through three shortened nights. Because they crossed the International Date Line, they lost a day, and thus their flight took just two calendar days. However, those two days included one extra night.

Recently a mother in the United States wanted to

telephone her son in Japan to wish him a happy birthday. When the connection was made, he was listening to her on his birthday, while she was speaking to him the day before. In fact, it could be truthfully said that she heard his answer the day before he spoke.

Fortunately, the meridian of the International Date Line crosses the Pacific Ocean. Wherever it passes over land, the line is bent and moved out to sea. It would be far too complicated to live in a country on the Date Line and be constantly losing and gaining days.

The selection of a great circle for a prime meridian and a date line was important not only to those who wished to standardize time but to all the men who sail the seas, fly the airways, or map the land. For all positions on either land or sea are given in terms of degrees of *longitude* east or west of the prime meridian.

Since the Sun appears to move in a westerly direction at the rate of 15 degrees each hour, time can be used to find positions on the Earth. Imagine, for example, that you were dropped down in the middle of a desert somewhere on Earth. With only a stick and a watch set accurately to Greenwich Time, you could find your longitude. Place the stick upright in the ground. When the shadow is shortest, it is noon, Solar Time, on your meridian. Now compare it with Greenwich Time. If it is after noon, Greenwich Time, you are west of Greenwich, England. If it is before noon, you are east of Greenwich.

Suppose it is 11 A.M., G.C.T. Then you are 1 hour × 15° from Greenwich, or 15° East Longitude. On a world map or globe, you will see that the meridian of 15° East Longitude passes through the Sahara Desert.

If your watch says it is 5 A.M., G.C.T., or seven hours before noon on the Greenwich meridian, your longitude is 7 × 15°, or 105° East. The map shows that you are in the Gobi Desert in Mongolia.

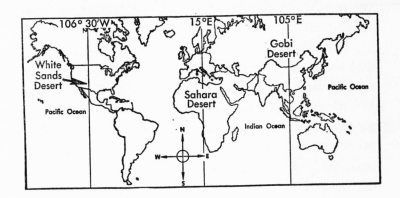

If it is six minutes after 7 P.M., G.C.T., or seven hours, six minutes (7.1 hours) after noon at Greenwich, your longitude would be 7.1 × 15°, or 106.5° West. On the map you will find that the White Sands Desert in New Mexico is located on the meridian which is 106.5°, or 106° 30′ West of Greenwich. But perhaps you already guessed where you were when you saw the great dunes of white gypsum "sand."

Even the people of the ancient world knew that it was possible to determine longitude by the difference between local time and time on a prime meridian. What they did not have was an accurate mechanical way to give them the time on the prime meridian. The invention of such a timepiece had to wait about 2,500 years until technical skills and materials were equal to the task.

If you stay on land, you may never need to find your longitude. After all, it is most unlikely that you will suddenly be dropped down in the middle of a strange desert. Generally, you know where you are. If not, you can ask someone, read a sign post, or tell by such landmarks as a familiar mountain or river. But the sailor at sea, or the aviator high above the clouds, has no sign posts nor handy policeman to ask. He must know his longitude. Early sailors used dead reckoning (see page 43) to determine longitude. On fairly calm seas, a sailor could estimate his position quite well by finding out how far and in what direction the ship had traveled. But tossing, stormy seas made it impossible to hold a steady course, and an error of even 1 degree of longitude at the Equator is equal to 69.65 miles.

After the defeat of the Spanish Armada in 1588, England became the greatest sea power in the world. With this power came the need for a better way to determine a ship's longitude at sea. In 1714, and for one hundred years thereafter, the "Commissioners for the Discovery of Longitude at Sea" offered a series of prizes for finding and improving ways to determine exact longitude. Many men worked on this problem, but the winner of the most important prize, about $100,000, was John Harrison.

Harrison was born in Yorkshire, England, in 1693. When very young, he worked with his father, who was a carpenter and also repaired furniture and clocks. Young John was very clever at making mechanical things and soon was building wooden works clocks. He tried constantly to improve clocks, and one of his inventions was the grid pendulum (see page 60).

Like other clockmakers of his day, Harrison was interested in the prizes offered by the commissioners, and he set to work on an accurate watch, or *chronometer* (kro·nahm'·eh·ter). The name "chronometer" comes from two Greek words meaning "to measure time." Harrison had no quick and easy success. He worked for more than thirty-three years before he had a timepiece ready to be tested. He was sixty-eight years old by then, too old to make the sea voyage to check his chronometer—but his son sailed in his place. The instrument was a success; it changed only one minute and five seconds in the five-month trip to the West Indies and back. Eight years later, after much further testing, Harrison finally was awarded his prize.

During the following thirty years many improvements were made in the chronometer. But for the next 150 years, the instruments used on board the great ocean liners were essentially the same as those made in the early 1800s. A new type of chronometer was perfected in 1957. It is ten times as accurate as the older type. Instead of being wound by a key, this new instrument gets its power from a motor driven by the vibrations of a tuning fork.

Most ships today still use the old style instruments. Big liners carry several chronometers. These are delicate instruments, and there are many rules about their care. Chronometers are set to Greenwich Time and can run fifty-six hours. It is customary, however, to wind them every twenty-four hours. On board ship, the care of the chronometer is usually assigned to one sailor, who reports to the captain after each winding. Chronometers are usually kept near the center of a ship, away from the engines, to protect them from vibrations and magnetism. Humidity, temperature, and air pressure are also controlled as far as possible.

With all this care, it is still important to check the chronometer often. Today's sailors can tune the ship's radio to one of the many stations which send out accurate time signals. The U.S. Naval Observatory furnishes this service over such stations as NNS in Annapolis, Maryland; NPG, Mare Island, California; and NPM, Pearl Harbor, Hawaii. Other nations offer similar services.

When there was no radio, it was the custom to check the chronometer before the ship left harbor. Sometimes odd methods were used to get the exact time to the sailor on board ship. In front of the castle in Edinburgh, Scotland, for example, there is a cannon which is fired each day at exactly noon. Ship captains in the harbor knew that the sound traveled 1 mile in five seconds and could check their chronometers accordingly.

A much more common time signal was a large ball hung high above the skyline of a port city. In the United States, until radios became common, the Western Union Telegraph Company closed its wires to all regular business at ten minutes before noon every day and began transmitting time signals from the U.S. Naval Observatory. Exactly at noon by these signals, the ball was dropped, and all over the harbor the chronometers on board ships were checked.

New York City still has a time ball in operation. High atop the Seamen's Church Institute on South Street at 11:45 each morning, a 4-foot black ball is raised to the top of a pole by a hand crank and held there by a magnet. At one minute to 12, as the time signals come over the telegraph wires from the Naval Observatory, the count down begins. At exactly noon, the magnet releases the ball and it slides to the bottom of its 15-foot pole. Very few chronometers are checked by this time ball any more, but office workers in the Wall Street area use it to set their watches, and the Seamen's Institute is swamped with telephone calls whenever the ball does not drop.

With the successful invention of the chronometer, man was able to measure space in terms of time. By accepting one meridian as the prime meridian, a starting point from which to measure was established. With this, plus a sextant to shoot the Sun and find the exact second of solar noon, man could find his position anywhere on Earth. But he also needed a starting point from which to find his position in time—a fixed point from which to count the years.

Each of us might say, "Time began for me when I was born." But it would mean very little to a stranger if you were to use the date October 12, 14, and your brother called it October 12, 8, while your father used the date October 12, 38. A single fixed point on which many people can agree is needed. Usually the best system of counting a long series of things is to start at the beginning. But when did time begin?

Different cultures and religions have different answers. All would agree, however, that the world was created before man appeared on this Earth, and certainly long before he learned to write or count. Since this natural starting point is lost forever in the past, another convenient point must be chosen.

Probably the first starting points were important local events. Just as you might say, "I know that happened three years ago because that was the year we moved into our new house," so ancient people also counted the years. Sometimes they counted from the year of the locust plague, sometimes from a great flood, or earthquake, and sometimes even from a small-pox epidemic. But as large nations were formed, local events were no longer enough. The great flood which ruined the crops in one part of the country might be unknown in another part. An event of national importance was needed.

The Greeks used the Olympic Games as a starting

point. One was held every four years. Each four-year period was called an *Olympiad* (oh·lim′·pee·add), and people spoke of such dates as the 2d year of the 31st Olympiad. The Romans used the date of the legendary founding of the city of Rome—*anno urbis conditae* (ah′·know er′·bis cone·dee′·tie), or simply A.U.C.—as their starting point. The French Revolutionary Government used the date it came to power to establish the Year 1. Even the new republic of the United States at one time dated documents from the Year 1 of the American Revolution.

Often the date was dependent on the reign of a king, or emperor. For example, people said that Christ was born in the twenty-eighth year of the reign of Augustus. This system was kept even after more general starting points were accepted. For many years it was the custom in the Catholic world to name the eras for the popes in Rome.

Antiques also are often dated according to kings and queens. We say a piece of furniture belongs to the period of King Louis XIV of France, or Queen Anne of England. The Latin word *circa* (sir′·kah), meaning "around," is sometimes used before the date of an antique. It means that the exact date is unknown, but that the piece was made sometime "around" that year. It is written *circa 1650*, or simply *c. 1650*, and is used whenever a date is uncertain.

The history of some ancient countries is divided into *dynasties*. A dynasty is a succession of rulers from the same family. There were thirty dynasties

123

in ancient Egypt. We still date Chinese art by the name of the dynasty in power when it was created. Some of the famous Chinese dynasties are:

Shang	c. 1523 B.C.	c. 1027 B.C.
Chou	1027 B.C.	256 B.C.
Ch'in	221 B.C.	207 B.C.
Han	202 B.C.	220 A.D.
Tsin	265 A.D.	420 A.D.
Sui	581 A.D.	618 A.D.
T'ang	618 A.D.	906 A.D.
Sung	960 A.D.	1279 A.D.
Yuan	1279 A.D.	1368 A.D.
Ming	1368 A.D.	1644 A.D.
Ch'ing	1644 A.D.	1912 A.D.

Even today, the British date official Acts of Parliament according to the ruler. Such an act might be dated "the fifth year in the reign of Queen Elizabeth II." These "regnal years" begin with the day the ruler assumes power.

Since the calendar was usually the concern of the priests, they often selected the starting point. The Biblical priests used the creation of man, which according to their calculations occurred on the date that would be listed as October 7, 3761 B.C., New Style. Moslem calendars date time from the Hegira (heh·jigh'·rah), Mohammed's flight from Mecca to Medina. The Year 1 of the Moslem calendar began on July 15, 622.

It was a learned monk who lived in the early part of the sixth century who chose the starting point which is most commonly used today. Dionysius Exiguus probably was born in ancient Scythia, which is now part of Soviet Russia. He came to Rome as a young man and soon was well known for his translations of books from Greek into Latin. He also wrote books on church law. It was this work which led to his interest in fixing dates.

Dionysius did not try to determine when time began. Instead, he decided to use an important event somewhere in man's long history as the starting point. And what could be more important than the birth of Christ! Of course, in those days there were no birth certificates, or other records, to show the exact date of a person's birth. Working more than five hundred years after the event, Dionysius was forced to do research in documents that were not always accurate. With the aid of some guesswork, he finally decided that Christ was born in the twenty-eighth year of the reign of Augustus, which was also the year 754 A.U.C. This became the year 1 A.D. under the system devised by Dionysius. A.D. stands for *anno domini* (ah'·know doh'·min·ee), which is Latin for "in the year of our Lord." Modern historians feel that Dionysius placed the birth of Christ four years too late. But considering how little he had with which to work, he made a very close estimate, and we still use his date.

Dionysius certainly chose a logical starting point for the Christian world. But since he was a great scholar, he could not ignore all the years before the birth of Christ. His solution was simple. He numbered those years backward from the great event.

125

The year 753 A.U.C. became the year 1 Before Christ, or B.C. The year 752 A.U.C. became 2 B.C., and so forth.

Historians have had good reason to be thankful to Dionysius for his system. Estimates of the length of the age of man on Earth have changed many times. Once it was believed that man first roamed the Earth about 5,700 years ago. Later historians pushed the date back to 25,000 years ago. The estimate given today varies from 100,000 to 1 million years. If a new starting date were needed for each new estimate, keeping track of dates would be very complicated indeed. But the system of Dionysius permits us to count the years in both directions and makes it very simple to add new information.

Dionysius' system was adopted almost immediately in most of Italy and Spain. About three hundred years passed before it was used in England, and the Catholic Church itself did not use this system until 400 years after the death of Dionysius. Today many nations use only the starting point chosen by Dionysius. Other countries, such as Japan, Israel, and India, have two or more calendars—one of which is the Gregorian—and therefore use several eras. The new Indian calendar went into effect on March 22, 1957 A.D., or Chaitra (chigh·trah) 1, 1879, Saka Era. Saka Era is named for the dynasty that ruled Northern India when the first scientifically prepared Indian calendar was introduced on March 22, 78 A.D.

THE YEAR 1960 A.D. TRANSLATED INTO
SOME OF THE OTHER ERAS

Era	Date
Byzantine	7468–7469
Hebrew	5720–5721
Olympic	2736, or the 4th year of the 684th Olympiad
Roman	2713 A.U.C.
Japanese	2620, or the 35th year of the period of Showa
Saka (India)	1881
Moslem	1380

The 7,469 years of the Byzantine Era seem like a long time compared to the life of one man. But it is hardly more than the brief tick of a clock when compared with the age of the Earth. Man is not content to record only the years of written history. Just as he is trying to push on into the space frontiers of the future, he is determined to push aside the curtains that cover the past. In laboratories and in the field, scientists are busy dating the great events of the prehistoric past.

9. Time Is Relative

At noon on New Year's Day, 1654, the Earth was exactly 5,658 years, 66 days, and 3 hours old. By 1900, the Earth was 100 million years old, and today, it is somewhere between 4 and 5 billion years old. Of course, the Earth did not age faster in the last hundred years, but wonderful new methods of estimating its age were discovered.

In 1654, James Ussher, an archbishop of the Church of England, declared that the Earth was created at nine o'clock in the morning of October 4, 4004 B.C. He based his estimate on his studies and interpretations of the Bible. Ussher was a very famous scholar, and his date was widely accepted. Some old copies of the Bible give his date of creation in a footnote. Of course, not everyone was willing to accept this date.

If Ussher had lived during the Middle Ages, his date probably would have been unchallenged for hundreds of years. Instead, his was an age when great scientific progress was being made, and men were questioning everything. Evidence against Ussher's date began to pile up. In 1715, Edmund Halley, the Astronomer Royal of England, for whom the famous comet is named, suggested a way to estimate the age of the Earth by the amount of salt in the ocean. Since it was known that the ocean became saltier each year, Halley recommended that the salt content be measured regularly.

James Hutton, who worked during the second half of the 1700s, is sometimes called the father of modern *geology*. A geologist is a scientist who studies the Earth. Hutton's plan of attack showed great common sense, even though many people in those days thought it strange. Instead of searching in the books of men, he proposed that scientists study the Earth itself if they wished to learn its history. This idea opened up a whole new field of science. Around the world men began to dig the Earth and keep and compare records. The remains of ancient life, which we call *fossils*, became scientific evidence.

From the beginning, it was obvious that 6,000 years was far too short a time to account for all the fossil remains on the Earth. Geologists examined and measured the *strata* or layers of rock. Soon it was noticed that certain fossils occurred only in one type of stratum. A geologic scale of time was devised, and names were given to the different periods. As more evidence was gathered, the estimated age of many of the periods was pushed farther and farther back in time. Perhaps more than once during your life, changes will be made in the dates on the geologic scale. The scale in the illustration shows the most recent estimates.

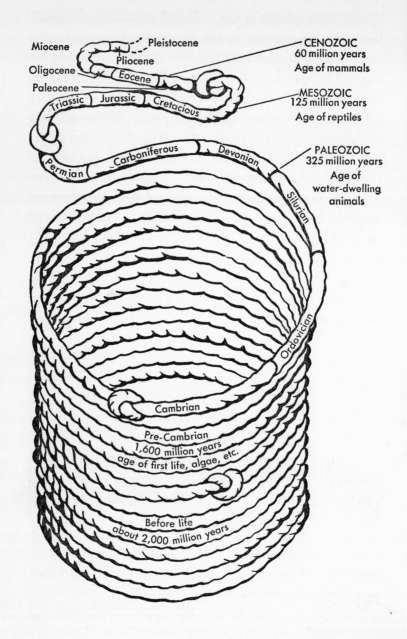

In a few places in the world, it is possible to count the years accurately by the layers in the rock in the same way that a woodsman tells the age of a tree he has cut by counting the rings in the trunk of the tree. In Switzerland, in 1865, Oswald Heer was studying the shale beds of the Miocene Period. He found that each layer of this rock bed was made up of three parts. On the bottom, there were blossoms of the poplar and camphor trees—a sign of spring. Next, he found fossils of winged ants and fruits of the elm and poplar—a summer sign. And in the final layer of shale, there were fall fruits of the camphor, wild grape, and date plum.

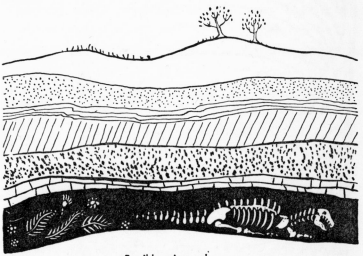

Fossil-bearing rock

A somewhat similar layer of shale was found in Green River, Wyoming. Here, each layer is divided into summer- and winter-fossil remains. Each layer is 7 one thousandths of an inch (.007) thick, and the entire shale bed is 2,600 feet in thickness. From these measurements, geologists figured that 6½ million years were needed to build this bed of oil-bearing shale.

Of course, there are very few places where the age of rock can be counted so accurately. But by using the known evidence and making many estimates, the geologists of the late nineteenth century figured that the Earth was about one hundred million years old.

Meanwhile, the *physicists*, the scientists who study the properties of matter, had been working on a different method of determining the age of the Earth. At that time, they believed that when the Earth was first created, it was a ball of hot gases which gradually cooled and became solid. The physicists based their estimate of the age of the Earth on the length of time it would take for the Earth's crust to cool. Their figures indicated that the Earth was much less than 100 million years old, and there were many arguments between the physicists and the geologists.

The physicists destroyed their own timetable when Marie Curie discovered *radium*, and the study of radioactive elements forged ahead. As radioactive elements break down, they give off heat. The scientists had not allowed for this heat in their early estimate of the cooling of the Earth's crust. Even though the discovery of radium destroyed the old method, it brought a new method of measuring time.

The radioactive element *uranium* will break down

14 per cent in 1 billion years; 12 per cent will become lead, and 2 per cent helium. By measuring the amount of lead in a piece of freshly mined uranium ore, it is possible to determine the age of the ore.

The results of the uranium-lead method were startling. Now the physicists said the Earth was about two *billion* years old, and the geologists cried that this was far too much. But still newer methods have been devised. Men learned to measure the breakdown of rubidium into strontium, and the breakdown of potassium into the gas, argon. These methods give the Earth an estimated age of from 4 to 5 billion years. Astronomers, working independently of the physicists, and geologists have come to the same conclusion. Today, most scientists accept the estimate of 4 to 5 billion years.

An interesting method has been worked out to find the probable age of fossils and other remains deposited between 1,000 and 50,000 years ago. *Radioactive carbon,* or carbon-14, is formed in the air by the action of cosmic rays. Living creatures breathe in this air, and the radioactive carbon is deposited in their bodies. The process stops at death, and the carbon-14 begins to break down. By measuring the breakdown, it is possible to determine the age of the remains. At present, there are only about ten laboratories in the world which are equipped to measure carbon-14 breakdown. One of these is located at the University of Arizona, which also has a Department of *Dendrochro-*

nology (den'·droh·kro·nahl'·oh·gee), the measurement of time as made from a study of the rings in a tree trunk. Dr. Edmund Schulman, Professor of Dendrochronology at the University of Arizona, is credited with finding the oldest-known living things, a group of bristlecone pine trees more than 4,000 years old. This is at least 900 years more than the age of the oldest-living sequoia tree in California.

Geologic strata, salt in the sea, the disintegration of uranium and carbon-14, the rings of a tree—all these are ways of measuring the amount of time which has passed. The swinging pendulum, the vibrating quartz-crystal, and the caesium atom count time in the present. But what happens to time when man leaves the Earth and travels out into space? For the role of time in the new "Space Age," we must turn again to the clock of the Universe.

All time is measured in terms of movement in space. One day is the length of time it takes the Earth to make one complete rotation on its axis, or the time it takes for any spot on the Earth's Equator to spin 24,902.39 miles around and return to its original position. One year is the time it takes the Earth to travel nearly 584 million miles through space in its orbit around the Sun.

Space is often measured in terms of time. The American Indians described the distance to a good hunting ground as "two moons' journey." We say: "Washington is four hours from New York by train." The distance from the Earth to a star, or the distance between stars, is measured in *light-years*. One light-year is the distance that light travels in one year. Since the speed of light is about 186,000 miles per second, and there are 31,536,000 seconds in a year, a light-year is nearly 6 million, million miles. Because even the nearest star is over four light-years away, it would be very clumsy to use miles to measure the distances in space.

Man measures distance on Earth in three ways. *Linear*, or measurement along a line, is in one dimension—length. *Plane*, or measurement of a flat surface, uses two dimensions—length and width. *Solid*, measurement of a solid object, uses three dimensions—length, width, and depth. Each of these measurements usually is made on an object that we may consider as standing still. It is true that all things and all people on Earth are spinning and whirling through space at a tremendous speed, but since every object is moving at the same rate of speed, each seems to be standing still with relation to any other object.

It is easy to understand this if you think of what happens when you are on a train. If your train is slowing down to pull into a station and another train passes at 70 miles an hour, its windows are just a blur, and there is no question in your mind that the other train is going very fast. But if each train is going at 70 miles an hour in the same direction, both trains seem motionless. You can look into the windows of the other train easily and see everything that is happening. Now if your train goes speeding on and passes the second train, which is slowing down, once more the windows are blurred and you know that your train is racing ahead.

The situation is somewhat the same when measurements are made in space. The rate of speed of each heavenly body may remain unchanged, but they differ from each other. Since each star is rushing outward from the center of the Universe at a tremendous rate, a *fourth dimension* is needed when measurements are made in space. This dimension is time.

Measurement in space has opened a great new field for discovery and exploration. It also has presented many new problems. Man needed to develop new systems of mathematics to deal with them. Some of the new questions and problems can be solved by the minds of mathematicians and scientists. Other problems must wait until space travel is a fact.

One problem often discussed is what will happen to the age of a man who is traveling rapidly through space. According to Albert Einstein, who developed the *theory of relativity*, time passes more slowly on a rapidly moving object than on one which is not moving as fast. Some scientists believe that a space traveler, moving almost as fast as the speed of light, would age only a few years during a round trip to Sirius, which is about 8.8 light-years away. At the same time, his twin brother who remained on Earth would grow about eighteen years older. Other scientists feel that space travel would make no difference; the body would age at the same rate under any conditions. Only space travel itself can show what will really happen.

Another part of the space-time relationship attracts science-fiction writers. The beam of light which you see tonight from the star Sirius left there 8.8 years ago. The light from some stars in our galaxy is thousands of years old before it reaches Earth. In the same way, light reflected from Earth travels outward in space. Some writers like to imagine a time machine which could cut through rays of Earth-light hundreds of light-years away in space and so see the happenings of the past. Since time is continuous, there may be some basis for the science fiction.

Einstein once summed up the continuity of time in a clever joke. Closing the door behind a guest who had overstayed his welcome, the great scientist remarked that "time is like a departing guest, always going, but never gone!"

Index

141

About the Authors and Artist

BEULAH TANNENBAUM was born in New York City, and after receiving her M.A. from Columbia University went to Cleveland, Ohio, to direct an educational research project in the public school system. Then she spent a year teaching in a French normal school before returning to New York as Science Specialist and Children's Librarian in the Ethical Culture schools of New York City. She has also been Science Consultant at the Downtown Community School in New York City. Mrs. Tannenbaum now lives in New Paltz, New York, with her husband, Professor Harold Tannenbaum, and their two sons—Robert and Carl.

MYRA STILLMAN was born in Albany, New York, and received her B.A. and M.A. there at the New York State College for Teachers. She has also attended summer sessions at Columbia University, Vassar, and New Paltz State Teachers College. She has been a teacher, librarian, and social worker in New York State—at the Westfield State Farms in Bedford Hills, at the County Welfare Department in Albany, and at Poughkeepsie Day School. Mrs. Stillman now lives in New Paltz, New York, with her husband, Professor Nathan Stillman, and their two sons—Robert and Michael.

WILLIAM D. HAYES was born in Goliad, Texas, sixty miles from San Antonio, and grew up around Phoenix, Arizona. Now a book illustrator, he lives in New York City, where he is associated with Scholastic Magazines.